Advanced Karate-Do

Advanced
Karate-Do

Dennis Wilton

The Crowood Press

Wiltshire SN8 2HR

British Library Cataloguing-in-Publication Data

A catalogue record for this book is available from the British Library.

ISBN 1 86126 293 0

Designed and typeset by Annette Findlay

Printed and bound by J W Arrowsmith, Bristol

Contents

Acknowledgements

The author would like to thank the following people for their help and support in the preparation of this book: designer Tony Wilton and his wife Clare (my daughter) for the illustrations, David Wilton (my son) for taking the photographs, Rei Sako for checking the Japanese dictionary, John Lovatt Sensei for his help and ongoing support, St Andrew's Church in the Westlands for allowing me to use the church hall for the photographs, and my wife Jennifer for helping with the photographs and supporting my work. I would also like to thank Jim Breen, Department of Digital Systems, Monash University, for the free download of a Japanese word processor and a collection of Japanese fonts; without these two contributions the dictionary would not have been possible.

Preface

THE PRIEST AND THE DIAMOND

A priest held out a piece of glass, cut and shaped like a diamond. The glass was fastened to a piece of thread which he held between his thumb and forefinger. Twisting the thread slowly, the glass rotated.

'What do you see?' he said to the man.

'A beautifully cut piece of glass with many sides,' replied the man.

'Yes! What else?'

'Each side reflects minute patches of light as the glass rotates.'

The priest moved to a nearby porthole in the temple wall, and again slowly rotated the glass. 'Now what do you see?'

'The light is now coloured by the blue of the sky.'

The priest took the man into another room where there were several lighted candles. 'Now what do you see?'

'The light has changed. The glass is now tinted with yellow, and reflects the flame of the candles.'

The priest held out the glass and offered it to the man, but as the man was about to take it the priest let it drop to the stone floor where it shattered into tiny fragments. The man was upset. He had admired the finely cut piece of glass and was distressed to see it destroyed.

'Why do you fret?' asked the priest. 'It was only a piece of glass!'

'Yes, but it was no ordinary piece of glass. It had been cut and polished, like a diamond.'

'Do you not see?' said the priest.

'See! I see fragments of something that was once beautiful but is now destroyed.'

'You saw, but you did not see.' He paused for a moment, then continued: 'The glass was one entity, the man. The sides were the sides of his personality. The colours were his moods. As the glass turns so does the personality, and the colours of its moods change with each environment. It radiates beauty and charm and gives great pleasure, but like the glass it can be shattered, and, indeed, must be shattered, for as attractive as it appears there lies within a greater treasure, which cannot be shattered, and its beauty outshines the glass a million-fold.' He pointed to the shattered remains. 'Look closely.'

As the man surveyed the splintered parts he saw a tiny stone, a diamond, of which the glass was merely a replica.

'This,' said the priest, 'is the real self, a priceless gem. When the light of the infinite catches the diamond it acts as a prism, reflecting the moods of the universe. The infinite life, with its greatness and vast beauty, can all pass through this small gem of self, a self which, ultimately, is not self, but part of a vast creation.'

Foreword

'If the quality of a person's life is changed for the better through the practice of karate, and they are able to share these benefits with their family and others, I am pleased.' These are the words of Shotokai Karate Master, Mitsusuke Harada. In this, his second book, Dennis Wilton has demonstrated a willingness to share with everyone the fulfilment he has found through the practice of karate. It takes courage to commit to writing one's thoughts and ideas on any subject; more so on a subject that is usually undertaken by notable masters. Courage is something that Dennis is not lacking, and any criticism levelled at his work will only serve to strengthen his resolve to go further into his study of karate.

The analysis of any subject or object is a delicate operation. It is a simple matter to break something down into its constituent parts; breaking down a karate kata into just a series of individual techniques could be done by any middle kyu grade, but to do this without losing the integrity of the whole kata needs a level of understanding that can only be achieved through many years of serious study. Dennis has applied to his study of karate the same dedication that has helped him achieve a professional level in several other subjects, such as photography and his university studies in which he achieved an Honours Degree.

If students who read his book gain a genuine insight into the art of karate-do, and go on to achieve their own personal standards, Dennis's work will have achieved its aim. What more could an author ask of his work. Read on!

John Lovatt

1 Introduction

In my previous book, *The Complete Book of Karate-do*, I set out to explain basic procedures in the dojo, and to provide a graphic description of techniques and kata. The book is complete in the sense that it contains all the essential kata required for white to black belt students. Additional kata are offered by several organizations and are sometimes referred to as 2nd or 3rd Dan kata, however it is preferable to think of them as an extended repertoire, as they include numerous techniques not covered by previous kata.

The purpose of this book is to explain some of the psychological values gained by using karate-do in a particular way, to discuss the nature of karate-do, and to expand on the notion of *Bunkai* (analysis of technique). The additional kata, twelve in all, are described and the techniques used in them are listed with photographic illustrations.

The foreword is written by one of the most qualified martial artists in Britain, John Lovatt Sensei. Sensei is qualified in several of the martial arts, and all his grades have been awarded by high-ranking Japanese masters. He holds the title of Renshi, is a 5th Dan Karate, 5th Dan Iaido, 4th Dan Kendo, 3rd Dan Jujitsu, and a 1st Dan Judo. Sensei was one of the first to study under Sensei Abbe before being handed over to Mitsusuke Harada, under whose instruction he was among the first to qualify as a Dan grade – black belt. I feel honoured that he has agreed to contribute the foreword to this book.

My attempts to explain psychological values in Chapter 2 may appear a little unorthodox, but are based on my research into the field of 'mind over matter'. People with illnesses, both major and minor, have gained considerable benefit from this type of approach, however I am unaware of anyone other than myself using karate-do in this manner.

The true nature of karate-do is often neglected in preference of the media interpretation, involving dazzling performances enhanced by the 'magic' of technology, and the appearance of individuals who can only be described as physical phenomena. Such images can be very discouraging to 'normal' people, who become convinced that karate-do is for the young, the very fit and for individuals who are prone to violence. My aim in Chapter 3 is to provide a down-to-earth approach to this very fine art form, and present it in a way that may appeal to anyone interested in pursing this practice.

Bunkai, or applied technique, is a very valuable part of karate-do training, and again, unfortunately, neglected in favour of competition sparring. As masters often return to *Taikyoku Shodan* as the ultimate training kata, I have, myself, returned to the basic, and in many ways the most advanced kata, *Taikyoku Shodan*, to explain some of the fundamental elements of this practice, and included parts of other kata to offer interpretation of various movements. It is essential that students develop control and effectiveness in the techniques they learn, as indiscriminate use may lead to prosecution and even imprisonment. Chapter 4 will help students come to terms with powerful techniques and encourage respect for others when using them.

The additional kata extend the repertoire of the student's knowledge. Often, students with a limited number of kata feel restricted in their knowledge of karate-do. Although the individual does not require knowledge of a great number of kata to perform well, or to qualify at high levels, there is still the need for access to these additional kata. Hopefully, the inclusion of twelve additional kata will bridge the gap felt by many students and lead them to a more fulfilled training practice.

2 Mind Over Illness

Many years ago someone said to me, 'If you could have anything in the world, what would it be?' Without hesitation I replied, 'The will to do whatever I set my mind to do!' This reply was surprising, most of all to myself; unwittingly I had realized the basis of my personal philosophy. There have been many projects I have successfully completed as a result of this philosophy, but the most challenging experience was a recent illness.

When I was nearing completion of *The Complete Book of Karate-do*, I did not realize that I had cancer. For most of 1997 I was plagued with tiredness, and tests showed that I had severe anaemia. On one occasion I was admitted to hospital for a blood transfusion. Being in my late fifties I assumed that age was making an early strike, and that the onus lay with myself to combat the increasing fatigue and weariness. Performing a single kata eventually made my body ache and burn and it became increasingly difficult to ward off apprehensions of physical limitations.

The more I fought against the illness the less I achieved, so the more I fought. I developed a stronger focus, and projected a mental image of age at every point in the kata, using all those splendid techniques to ward off this predator. My aim was to prove to myself that I was able, and unprepared to accept the twilight years so easily. I encouraged myself with thoughts of Master Funakoshi who trained and taught karate-do into his eighties. I also remembered other *karateka* older than myself who were still practising and keeping well. I intended to be one of them.

However, by Christmas 1997 I had developed severe abdominal pains. They were so bad that I could no longer stand or care for myself. On Monday 29 December my doctor arranged for an ambulance to take me to the City General Hospital where, after several tests, they diagnosed a tumour in the bowel which warranted immediate surgery. Within a few hours they were operating, and later that night I was recovering in the ward.

The following day I was informed that the tumour was in fact a cancer and that half of my large bowel and part of my intestine had been removed. I was later told that my body had done an excellent job of fighting off the disease and containing the cancer. At this point I reflected on my fight against age and felt confident that my efforts had contributed to my well-being.

This attitude of mind prevailed throughout my illness and saw me through many a desperate hour. Five weeks after surgery I was teaching in my club once again. Unable to perform or demonstrate, I sat on a chair advising and encouraging my students. Two weeks after that I was in my Gi, slowly and carefully working my way through kata. This improved my confidence and helped me overcome the depressing thoughts of disability. If all else fails, I thought, at least I will be able to teach, and in my own way I can perform the kata which have been so important in my life.

My aim now is to further develop my focus, not just to improve technique but to strengthen my mind. I was informed that the cancer could return in the future and that a thirty-week course of chemotherapy would hopefully prevent that from happening. To assist the drugs I therefore turned to the power of the mind.

I associated cancer with Ninja. The Ninja of Japan were silent killers, hired assassins who would use any means, usually foul, to kill to order any male, female or child. Anonymity was of paramount importance, making them masters of disguise. They were practised in medicines and expert in the use of poisons. They were void of pride, dignity or respect – except perhaps amongst themselves – and were the most deceitful of all fighters. How well this description fits a cancer!

I imagined placing the Ninja at every point in the kata, and began fighting them off. Although in reality I would have been out-matched, in the mind all things are possible. In my imagination I had ultimate awareness; I could sense them thinking and anticipated their moves. Like cancer cells hiding in the body, I saw the Ninja as shadows in a darkened room. I listened intently for the slightest sound or the flashing of a blade and responded instantly. At the end of the kata I assumed my victory, and a door opened through which came a cleansing surge of energy in the form of light. The energy washed away the disease, and the bodies of the Ninja were disintegrated and blown away by the wind. At this point I presented myself with the choice of relaxing or going through the door to meet my next challenge in the form of another kata.

I found this practice invigorating and positive – I was doing something for myself. Psychologically, though, it was a difficult task. In kata I was using karate-do, the 'way of the empty hand', while the Ninja had weapons, including swords, daggers, arrows and darts.

The idea of weapons helped enormously when interpreting technique, however. The slight angling of the body when performing a forearm block became an evasive movement against the downward sweeping of a sword or piercing arrow. A rising forearm block was used against the Ninja drawing a sword from behind. As this scene was of my own making, I also set the parameters. One of these parameters was a deadly rule that the shame of failure would make the Ninja commit suicide by drinking a self-made poison. My aim, therefore, was to be as stealthy as possible, using my self-endowed powers of awareness and skill. By introducing the act of suicide I absolved myself from the responsibility of killing the Ninja. Although death can result from applied technique, the kata were not really designed for that purpose. I certainly preferred innocence to guilt, even in my imagination, and suicide was a fairly common practice in ancient Japan.

To retain the form of the kata I set a second parameter: the Ninja could only attack within the structure of the kata. Attacking at any other time would bring shame and thus their demise. This left me free to work constructively on the form of the kata, and make each movement play a vital part in defeating the Ninja.

The surgeon told me that my condition would be monitored for at least three years, and if the cancer had not returned after that period there was a good chance that the battle had been won. Fighting the Ninja in kata, therefore, was an ongoing project. Kata are a major part of the art of karate-do and their integrity must be maintained, however. Confidence in the use of technique can only be gained through actual partner work. It would be immoral and against all decency to superimpose the Ninja image on to partners in practice. I therefore divided my kata practice into two parts: in the dojo classes I would practise kata in the traditional form, and in private I would fight the Ninja.

Remarkably, fighting the Ninja in private had a cleansing quality. There was a healthy sense of achievement and well-being, an inner silence. I could gauge my timing, start the kata when I felt ready and concentrate as much or as little effort as I needed. There was no confusion between the imagined and the real, and the danger of causing actual bodily harm was not an issue. This was a fantasy, a kind of virtual reality in which the 'Off' switch was always accessible. If I was interrupted, or felt the need to escape, there was no problem. In reality the practice was beneficial as it helped to sharpen the wits, increase awareness and improved my response to an attack.

The most attractive part of this type of kata practice is that it can be a purely mental activity, and there are many advantages to this. Sleepless nights can be spent mentally working through kata. At a subliminal level the mental conditioning helps to develop a conscious awareness and carries over to the practice in the dojo. In fact, whenever there is a quiet period, the mind can take on this silent activity, and of course the subject can be something other than the Ninja/cancer. Fears, phobias, and various types of infections can also be personified and placed at points in the kata. In this way the kata becomes a personal weapon. Through the use of this weapon, and the practice of traditional karate-do, there is no end to what can be achieved.

The picture painted so far is that kata practice is a very sober one indeed. This is true of martial arts generally. The media portrays a great deal of violence and bloodshed, accompanied by severe injury and often death. Competition fighting plays a key role in people's perception of the arts, and very often students enter clubs thinking they are going to learn wondrous flying kicks. My response to this is usually: 'You learn how to fly, and I'll teach you how to kick!'

3 The Nature of Karate-do

Respect for other people's safety is no longer taken for granted in any area of life; even the most respected of people, those in the caring professions, are showing concern. Doctors are wary of night time emergency calls; district nurses place themselves in vulnerable situations; and nannies and nurses often put themselves at risk. It is a sad fact that nowadays no one can be confident of their safety, and while this may sound alarmist, it is nonetheless true.

Although society protects us when the law is broken, avoiding these crimes and keeping ourselves safe from harm is an individual matter. Some intended victims have shown great presence of mind and the ability to defend themselves, and because of this have been spared the pain and indignity of assault. Karate-do, a philosophy as well as a martial art, contains all the requirements for self defence. The student does not have to be strong, aggressive or even young. Under the guidance of a qualified instructor, all the techniques will become natural and will prove extremely effective.

Unlike its portrayal in films and stories designed to fire the imagination with impossible feats, karate-do requires dedication and endless repetition – there are no overnight wonders. There is no easy way to deal with aggression, and along with the body, the mind needs conditioning; all the

techniques in the world will fail if fear grips the mind. The study of karate-do, therefore, is not simply a physical practice to develop prowess in the dojo, but a training of the mind and a discovery of self.

Kata vary in complexity, and in their simplest form involve the practice of techniques in various directions and postures in a choreographed form. All kata have their own character and interest, and each of them include different or varied techniques. It is unnecessary for the practitioner to study all of them.

Like kata, practitioners have different or varied preferences and needs. While some favour contact sports, others favour the technical or aesthetic aspects of karate-do. There are also those who find an expression of spirituality in the form and practice of kata. Whatever the character or disposition of the individual, there is something of value in karate-do for everyone wishing to pursue the art.

Although it would be a misconception to confuse karate-do with dancing, dancers also tread a path paved with hardship and dedication, and karate-do practitioners can learn a great deal about body management (*Tai Sabaki*) from studying them. Their dependence on focus, balance and quality of performance is no less significant than that of karate-do. Several styles of karate-do emphasize smooth, soft flowing movement along with the power and proficiency of technique. Relaxation and calmness of mind are essential elements in all performing arts, and kata are an excellent means of developing these qualities.

Emphasis on fighting and 'breaking' techniques is misleading. As with all performing arts, what is seen publicly is only a smattering of the skills of the performer and the art. How does one learn to kill except by killing? How does one learn to break bones except by breaking bones? Films are constantly showing these aspects of all the martial arts, and yet except in times of war or severe circumstances, who would do such things?

Karate-do is an art, a graceful and pure form of human activity. It is beneficial, not psychologically crippling; it is realistic, not fanciful; it is living history, and, as well as a means of defence, it is a path of discovery. Much of the training lies in kata practice, and partner work is used to test the techniques learned; if students fail here, they have failed in the kata. The value of the techniques depends on the person applying them. In partner work, sincerity and trust are of utmost importance because it is here that the techniques are tested in preparation against a real attack. Qualified supervision is required for safety and effectiveness.

The nature of karate-do is such that it requires the body to move in all directions and is a good all-round physical fitness routine. Without the need for excessive workouts karate-do acts on the cardiovascular system, tones the muscles and develops suppleness.

A kata can be performed in less than a minute. As the repertoire increases these forms can be practised quickly or slowly, gently or vigorously, and for as long as is required depending on the individual.

Unlike most exercise, in karate-do all the movements are designed for self defence and are of lifelong benefit to the practitioner. Karate-do uses natural movements which are the same for both men and women, and it would be a misconception to think that practising karate-do leads to the development of a masculine physique.

The most essential element in all self defence is awareness. Awareness involves timing and distance as well as an understanding of the immediate surroundings. Being aware of the person nearby and understanding their intended actions are two different entities. When proficiency is finally attained it is essential to remember that it is illegal to use any acquired technique against a person who is not an assailant. Even then, only sufficient force is allowed to prevent injury to oneself. When the offence stops, the defence must also stop. Such principles must be learned in the dojo at the start of training.

Teaching the martial arts requires a profound understanding of the chosen art. It is insufficient to simply explain in detail the physical action of a technique; there is a need to explain why the technique is performed in a particular fashion and why it is effective when performed properly. Furthermore, there is a need to appreciate the different ways in which people interpret information. The classic example of this is the story of three witnesses standing at different perspectives to an accident. Each in turn gave very different descriptions of the same accident. The fact is that we all see and interpret things differently, and persuading the student to see and understand the teacher's art is an art in itself.

It is sometimes thought that a student who struggles to perform is ill-equipped for this type of activity. It is important to remember that students have equal, but not necessarily the same, capabilities. Failure to understand this is ultimately a reflection on the poor quality of teaching. Standards, therefore, are extremely important, and karate-do exponents who are in a position to maintain those standards must do everything possible to improve the quality of teaching.

In karate-do, individuals are, more often than not, chosen to teach by teachers themselves. In this way standards are unlikely to drop, as the teachers will, through their own observations, recognize an individual's ability to teach. There are, however, a minority who elect to open clubs and teach without having any credentials or experience, and no qualified person to guide them. It is in these circumstances that reputations falter; students undergo bad experiences and express these to other would-be students. Such students rarely forget their experience; it colours their attitude, and by association tarnishes the work of qualified teachers.

In many dojos there is little reference to the spiritual values of the art. Emphasis is placed more on the physical aspects and sparring in the belief that this will prepare students for the real world. Unfortunately, there is little resemblance between the dojo and reality. In the dojo there are limitations – the opponent stops short of actual bodily harm. Reality provides no such security. An attacker who is worse the wear for drink or drugs, or is psychotic, is very hard to predict. Undeterred by a bloody nose or a cut lip, the attacker can be surprising and devious, catching the defender off-guard with serious consequences. Preparing a student in the dojo for reality, therefore, is an impossible task.

The natural ability of students to defend against attack varies considerably. While some are timid and easily intimidated, others are aggressive and eager to fight. Clearly, caution is needed when teaching students of such varied abilities. A timid student pitted against an aggressive partner will fail to thrive, and an aggressive student venting frustration will dominate the class. In each case a different approach is needed by the teacher.

Competition and self defence are only two reasons why people study karate-do. Others study to develop the mind or to gain insight into the spiritual values of Buddhism and Zen, or even for personal religious aspirations. They too have a right to tuition. Although the term 'martial art' presupposes combat of some sort, it must be remembered that most of the martial arts are living history. Weapons are now illegal, and the few weapons' techniques that remain, arguably within the law, are certainly unacceptable when used indiscriminately. The martial arts, therefore, must provide a vehicle of expression for a variety of philosophies and religions, and a teacher without knowledge of such matters would be inadequate in the eyes of the students.

Understanding the spiritual values of the martial arts makes students more aware, and probably more capable of evasive rather than defensive techniques. Self defence is a last resort and should rarely become a necessity; by being aware and cautious of circumstances, most dangerous situations can be avoided. Weak traits of human nature, such as pride and vanity, are usually instigators of conflict. They create turmoil and confusion and prevent natural response. Stronger traits such as humility and understanding provide a firm basis for defence as calmness and common-sense prevail.

Spiritual values, therefore, form the backbone of the martial arts. Prowess in the dojo means nothing if in reality the mind falters. Overcoming the barriers we face in the 'real world' is a precedent. Each individual has value. It is the responsibility of the teacher and the student to find that value and enhance it through tuition and practice.

4 Bunkai and Kata Design

Bunkai, the application of techniques, is probably the most important aspect of interpretation. Through *Bunkai* it is possible to experiment and diversify the use of kata. However, when students begin this practice there is a tendency to be led away from the form and pattern of the kata. The first movement of *Taikyoku Shodan*, for example, requires an individual to turn to the left and perform a left downward low-level forearm block while stepping to the left with the left foot. This is followed by stepping through to make a strike. When trying the *Bunkai* for the next movement, stepping through to make a right fist strike, a problem arises in how to pass the attacker just blocked. The attacker would have to mysteriously disappear.

This problem is often encountered in kata, and trying to resolve the problem can lead to changes in the kata form and pattern. However, form and pattern are required to preserve uniformity and a continuity of kata history. For various reasons masters and *karateka* have already invoked change, and kata practised in one part of the world may well be different from kata practised elsewhere. These changes can be the result of regarding the kata as a prototype, so that when the actual practice begins, changes in direction and performance of technique are altered to suit the situation. There is no fault in this idea.

Often the changes are minor and the kata retains it integrity.

Kata integrity, however, must be a concern for anyone working on interpretation through *Bunkai*. Obviously, the simplest way to resolve the problem of the second movement in *Taikyoku Shodan* is to introduce a strike immediately after the block. By doing this we dispose of the first attacker and are free to move to the next part of the kata. However, the integrity of the kata would be lost, and eventually this line of thought would lead to a complete revision of the form and pattern of the kata.

Another solution to the problem is to use the movement of the left foot to step to the inside of the attacker's leg and frustrate confirmation posture of stance and balance. By doing this the attacker may fall to the left leaving the way clear to step forward to make the movement.

A bolder interpretation could be made which necessitates correct body posture and movement. At the start of the kata, the defender and attacker may be face to face with the attacker taking hold of the defender's left wrist. By stepping to the left and thrusting the left fist down into a low-level block, the wrist would be released. If the attacker's grip is strong, there is the possibility that the body movement and thrusting action of the defender will throw the attacker to one side, and they will fall to the floor. The attacker may maintain his balance, however, and has therefore been pulled around to face the defender from the left. The distance between them will be too great to make a strike, which means that the defender may now make the movement forward with the right foot, strike the attacker and complete the first section of *Taikyoku Shodan*. In this way the integrity of the kata is maintained.

However, the objection could be made that the first movement of *Taikyoku Shodan* is a downward block rather than a releasing movement, and of course this objection is valid. If it is assumed that the first movement is a downward block only, the interpretation must observe this rule. How then does the defender step forward after the first block? It could be that the attacker's strike was taken sooner than was anticipated, and as a consequence the attacker began to move backward in an attempt to avoid the defender. The defender, however, steps through and makes the strike. This interpretation leaves the kata unspoiled.

Does this mean that kata are broken down into sections? The last interpretation would suggest that the first downward block, followed by stepping through and making a strike, is a complete section. In other words, a complete defence has been achieved in that the strike following the block did not leave the defender vulnerable. Interpretation depends to a large extent on how kata are assessed. For example, is each technique a separate item, which are then linked to form a kata? Does the pattern itself have any significance in the performance of the kata? Invariably kata end at the starting point, which is convenient in the sense that repositioning is not required at the start of each kata. Is this the only significance of the pattern?

If this is so, why do complicated patterns emerge?

Perhaps the pattern, along with the form, adds interest through complexity in the sense that kata become progressively more challenging. If this is the case then pattern serves a greater purpose than that of simply linking techniques. Is it likely that masters, appreciating that body movement itself was as much part of technique as the block or strike, catered for this in the pattern? This certainly offers a more attractive approach to understanding kata. Clearly proficiency in movement adds impetus to the technique itself and therefore has equal importance.

Returning to *Taikyoku Shodan* with these thoughts in mind, the next movement is a 180-degree turn. In its simplest form this action involves a change in direction. However, the way in which this turn is made indicates the importance of the pattern of movement. To turn 180 degrees into an oncoming attack is a bold action requiring courage. This is often overlooked when performing kata in a safe environment. Turning in such a situation requires precision in balance, distance, timing and technique. The turn, therefore, is crucial to the understanding of the kata and its interpretation.

One interpretation involves sweeping the leg around in a clockwise direction when making the turn, with the intention of unsteadying the attacker by stepping across the path of the oncoming stance. However, practice in *Bunkai* showed that the defender was more likely to fail than succeed when attempting to unbalance the attacker. The main cause of failure was that the line of balance in the defender's body was off-centre, making him weak and unsteady. The limited number of successes were unsatisfactory and depended on excellence of timing; if the sweeping foot crossed the attacker's path at exactly the right time the sweep was reasonably successful. In all, the result of the practice was an unreliable movement and a lack of confidence on the part of the defender.

In *The Complete Book of Karate-do* I suggested placing an additional attacker behind the defender to improve posture and balance. Rather than sweeping the leg around in a clockwise direction, I suggested that the defender drove his upper body backward into the attacker's grasping arms, thus disabling the attack. This action proved to be very successful. By driving backward into the arms of the attacker, the defender is striking at the abdomen of the attacker and weakening the offence. However, this action is not an attempt to change the kata by adding technique, but is designed to emphasize body movement when turning, and to show how vital it is to move correctly with good timing and distance.

Through this action the defender remained stable. Technique was positive and the integrity of the kata was maintained, since there is no evidence to show that sweeping the leg around in this fashion is an integral part of the kata. The movement reinforced the notion that the pattern of kata has as much significance as technique. Correct body movement through turns and direction are a fundamental part of technique in kata and add natural power to the technique. Furthermore, it indicated that kata are not simply techniques linked together to form a pattern of movement. Attacks can be multiple and come from any direction. Being able to turn and counter such an attack confidently is obviously desirable. The *Bunkai* for this movement in

Taikyoku Shodan, therefore, is evidently important.

Having completed the first section of the kata, the defender moves on to the second section, however the attacker is obstructing the defender's need to move forward to make a strike and thus fulfil the requirements of the kata. It could be said that seeing the first attacker dealt with so proficiently and powerfully, the second attacker is slightly hesitant. Not all attackers are defiant, and some are dealt with easier than others, but one can never assume an easy victory. It is essential that all students work to find their own interpretations without affecting the integrity of the kata. Understanding kata is as much a mental exercise as a physical one. It must be remembered that there are many interpretations, and the degree of understanding through practice relies greatly on the endeavour of the student.

In the next section the defender turns 90 degrees to perform a low-level block and three successive strikes. Here again the turn is not simply a change in direction. It requires all the elements of the 180-degree turn: precision in balance, distance timing and technique.

But why are three successive forward strikes necessary. If only one strike was used the kata would be shorter and use less space. The masters, however, proposed three strikes, which indicates again the importance of movement and the pattern of the kata. Being able to strike while moving forward is an essential part of karate-do, and including this in the *Bunkai* practice is extremely beneficial. All three steps are equal in the kata but may not be so in reality. One interpretation here is that the attacker, realizing impending danger, decides to retreat. The defender, using timing and distance, advances, makes a strike, advances again and makes another strike, and, finally, having gained in distance and taken the initiative away from the attacker, makes the third, telling strike.

Although this interpretation appears quite simple, it is in fact complex. To maintain body posture in this forward attacking motion requires considerable practice. It is essential in *Bunkai* that partners work in real terms, that is the attacker must make every effort to avoid the three strikes, while the defender must make every effort to gauge the distance and timing of the retreating attacker. It becomes evident through practice that any one of the strikes may be the 'telling' one, and the assumption that the last strike is such is invalid. It is wise to place this *Bunkai* practice within the kata itself. There is a tendency for partners to overestimate the distance required and fail to fulfil the kata requirements. In other words, it becomes an individual practice rather like *Sambon Kumite* (three-step sparring). Performing at least the next two sections in addition to the three strikes will maintain the integrity of the kata and avoid deviations into personal practice.

With the above thoughts in mind, *Bunkai* practice develops an appreciation of movement in kata. We cease to think of kata as a linking of techniques or an on-going battle. They become challenging and stimulating, and no matter how many times they are performed, something of interest will always be discovered. For example, one might ask why there are so many lines and directions in kata; why not a simple cross drawn on the floor to step on while individual techniques are performed? Perhaps floor space itself is significant; obviously attackers move about, and can approach from any direction. Being able to

use floor space intelligently is thus clearly an advantage. In the centre line of *Taikyoku Shodan*, perhaps the defender is not only driving one attacker away but also creating distance from attackers approaching from the rear!

The turn at the end of the three strikes may also be significant. Often a defensive move is made by turning away from or into the attack, as in *Irimi* (the ability to step into and slightly to the side of an attack), and being able to perform a technique while turning is vital. This is a strategic evasion and requires some degree of courage when working with proficient practitioners. *Irimi* is an excellent practice, and when done skilfully can deceive the attacker, for example using a forward movement the defender steps slightly to the side and past the attacker and moves out of the attacker's vision: it creates the illusion of disappearance.

Additionally, the strikes made in any kata can never be assumed to be effective. How many participants in competitions have incurred injury and even fractures with the contenders continuing to battle on afterwards? This is an important fact to remember when performing kata: we would be ill-advised to assume every strike is successful. Quite the contrary, in fact; it is difficult to disable with one strike, and even then the opportunity must be there. The significance of pattern in kata, with reference to the strategy of evasive movement therefore, is valid.

The pattern of the kata, however, is often spoiled by anticipating one move while performing another. This often happens, for example, at the end of the centre line in *Taikyoku Shodan*. The right foot in the *Zenkutsu Dachi* (front stance) is angled inward in preparation for the following movement. The final strike, therefore, was negative. If the third strike is ineffective the next movement is hardly likely to take place as the attacker would have the advantage. In any kata the blocks and strikes must be effective otherwise the practice is a pointless succession of fancy movements.

One might also ask why are there so many stances and techniques. These too are part of the kata pattern and design. Often, basic footwork is used in sparring, and the number of techniques are reduced to cater for individual preferences. In kata, however, all techniques are practised equally. Although a great number of techniques are steeped in history, and appear to be impracticable, in kata all have the same significance. *Nukite* (spear hand), for example, was originally used to penetrate the flesh, ribs, and the spaces between the body armour worn by the Samurai. Aside from it being illegal, it would be unthinkable to use such a technique in modern times. However, the kata retains them all and uses them in a variety of stances.

To a large extent, understanding kata is an individual process. Dwelling on the varieties of interpretation would reduce the class to an academic level with little actual training. The individual needs to begin asking hypothetical questions such as: 'Why is *Shuto Uke* (knife hand block) nearly always executed in *Kokutsu Dachi* (back stance)?';

'What advantage does *Neko Ashi Dachi* (cat stance) have? Clearly, such stances and techniques have value else why would the kata retain them. Also, 'Can all these techniques be used in sparring?' Indeed they should be, and the conscious inclusion of the various techniques and stances adds interest to sparring, and helps to guide the student away from pure competition to practical training.

Perhaps the biggest question in *Bunkai* is: 'Why are we learning all these techniques'? We live in far less hazardous times than the ancient Japanese, when failure to observe the superior rank of a Samurai could result in a beheading. Most of modern life is taken up with work, achievements, family matters and social intercourse, and prowess in the dojo has little significance. Even war has become hi-tech, and siege has become mostly a matter of negotiation.

Perhaps such questions bring us back to the fact that kata are living, moving history, and just as historians strive for the authenticity of the past, so must martial artists strive to maintain the integrity of the kata, for in them lies the character of the past. The bottom line is that all kata have significance, and to work through them regardless of their meaning would be futile. Only when true art shows has mastery been achieved.

5 Double Attacks

Double attacks are essential to the practice of karate-do, and add impetus to the realism of the art.

This is initially a three-person practice. One person stands at a centre point, and two others stand to either side. The first person faces forward, and the other two direct their attention to the sides of the person in the centre. The central person stands in the ready posture, *Yoi*, and the other two assume a front stance, *Zenkutsu Dachi*. Beginners to this practice find it easier to start with one attack, followed by the other, but as progress is made the attacks can be made simultaneously or at random.

Double attacks put the central person under some degree of pressure, and as a result certain habits begin to form. Initially, the central person focuses first on one attacker then on the other. When this happens, an attacker from the left may easily take the initiative while the central person's focus is on the right. It is essential therefore that the central person has an all-round focus, and this requires some practice. To develop this type of focus, look directly ahead and allow the sight to fall out of focus. While concentrating on the blurred images, become aware of the sight to the side – the old expression is 'looking through the corners of the eyes'. An impression of the attackers to either side will be seen and the ability to sense when one attacker is about to make an attack will be developed. This practice requires patience and many repetitions, and it may be months before any real progress is seen.

The three people are positioned in a straight line:

```
> ------------- | ------------- <
```

Often the central person subconsciously moves slightly off the line by shuffling backward to get a better view of the attackers. This should be avoided as positioning on the line adds impetus to the practice, and eventually heightens sensitivity.

When an attack takes place, the central person has a tendency to jump a little before moving to make a defence. This is due largely to the surprise of the attack and the eagerness to avoid being struck. Rather than increasing the speed of response to an attack, however, this initial movement impedes defensive tactics. The movement should be as natural as possible, as if someone was calling from a distance. In response to the call a simple turn would be made, followed by a natural walking movement towards the caller. It is essential to capture this feeling of movement when responding to the attack. A natural movement will be faster and the response smoother. Although one could hardly describe the rest of the movement as 'walking', the initial response is the same.

A similar response can be achieved by pressing the feet downward and outward while standing in the ready posture. This does not require movement in the feet, but is rather a feeling of pressure. By pressing the feet downward and to the sides, simply lifting one foot will initiate a movement sideways. Through practice and control of the pressure, a movement can be made in whichever direction is required.

Beginners usually make the mistake of stepping backward before making a defensive response. This movement, however, can easily be seen by the attacker who simply redirects the attack, making the defence difficult. To avoid this error, step to the side of the attacker. This takes a little courage but it soon becomes evident that it enables the central person to avoid the attack better. Ideally, the movement brings the central person to the side, and out of sight, of the attacker. This serves two purposes: firstly, the central person is able to defend confidently by attacking to the ribs or kidneys of the attacker, and secondly, the central person has successfully created greater distance between himself and the other attacker which allows a little more time to defend against the attacks.

Attackers can be deceptively fast, and any delay will result in failure. It is vital, therefore, that the first attacker is dealt with proficiently and a turn is made to defend against the second attacker. Defensive techniques need to be simple. A fist, elbow or knee strike should be sufficient to deter the first attacker, and in the following instant the second attacker must be dealt with. Even if the second attacker has, for whatever reason, failed to attack, it is necessary to be prepared.

When the second attacker has been dealt with, beginners tend to relax and try to analyse what has happened. Assuming the reality of the situation, there is no time at all to relax. Awareness and attention must be constant. When the two attackers have relented and are assuming their position for the next attack, the central person accepts the end of one attack and instantly prepares for further attacks until the end of the session.

Many students working on double attacks tend to wait for a movement from one of the attackers before responding. More advanced students tend to sense when the attack is about to take place. Often they move at the same time as the attacker, and in some cases slightly before the attacker. This has the effect of creating more time for the central person, and thus enables a more effective response. The ability to sense an attack should be included in all partner work, whether it be double attacks, *Ten No kata*, or sparring. In all walks of life, the ability to anticipate events predisposes success.

6 First Aid and the Martial Arts

This chapter does not constitute a course on first aid. Its main purpose is to make people aware of the need for a qualified first aider to be present at a karate session, and to encourage those who read it to qualify by attending a certified first aid course. In all sports there is the possibility of accidents. They may be minor, such as a splinter in the foot, or major, such as a heart attack. No matter what the injury is, there should be someone on-hand to deal with the situation. It is essential that all instructors/Sensei are trained and qualified in first aid.

Karate-do is an art requiring dedication and commitment in order to achieve any degree of personal achievement. Quite often the level of commitment, and consequently enthusiasm, may lead to mistakes resulting in an accident. In the attempt to achieve personal reward students often find they have stubbed a toe, bruised an arm or grazed the knuckles. Other overzealous students may train too hard, putting strain on the heart which results in a heart attack. Sometimes students can be unaware of a medical condition which may be induced for the first time through training.

Many students travel abroad, indeed karate-do is a worldwide activity, and I have therefore included a section on anaphylactic shock, which is caused by ingestion of certain types of unusual food and drink, snake bites, and stings, and results in a severe reaction in the casualty which can be very serious.

If there is no qualified first aider available to deal with the predicaments outlined, the student is left in a very precarious condition, and the organizers stand a good chance of being discredited.

THE MAIN PRINCIPLES OF FIRST AID

Preserve life – this requires attention to the airway, breathing and circulation.
Prevent a condition worsening – control bleeding, support fractures, and cool burns.
Promote recovery – reassure the casualty, get help, and protect the casualty from the elements.

The following guidelines should be observed:

• assess the situation
• diagnose the injury or condition – what happened, how it happened and when
• find out the symptoms – how does the casualty feel? Use the senses – look, listen and feel
• give immediate, adequate treatment
• arrange for the 'disposal' of the casualty – hospital, doctor or home
• remain calm throughout, reassure the casualty and control the situation.

Asthma attack

When an individual is suffering an asthma attack, they will have difficulty breathing, and there may be wheezing, difficulty in speaking, grey blue skin, and a dry tickly cough. Most asthma sufferers carry an inhaler with them, but some forget, and without proper treatment the condition deteriorates and can become very serious.

The first two points to remember are not to lay the casualty down, and not to use a 'preventer' inhaler (usually a brown colour). Make the casualty as comfortable as possible and offer reassurance. Allow the casualty to find their own most comfortable position; they usually find that sitting slightly forward is best. Although the casualty may be struggling to breath normally, encourage slower, deep breaths. Help the casualty to find the 'reliever' inhaler (usually a blue colour). Allow the casualty to use the inhaler, which should take effect within minutes. If the attack stops within ten minutes, encourage the casualty to use the inhaler again and to breath slowly and deeply. If the attack was severe, or if it was their first experience of an attack, tell the casualty to inform the doctor.

In the event that the casualty falls unconscious, be prepared to resuscitate them (*see* Resuscitation, page 32). If the inhaler fails to have any effect after ten minutes, dial 999, or ask someone else to call for an ambulance. It is essential to monitor the pulse and breathing until the casualty recovers or the ambulance arrives. Do not leave the casualty alone.

Back injury

Back injury may occur from a sudden jolt, such as a kick from the rear, or from a sudden twisting action

It is difficult to tell if someone has fractured the spine. There may be pain in the back or neck and tenderness when touched, or when someone lies down there is often a slight arch in the lower back. It is possible to slide one hand under this arch and gently feel for deformities in the alignment of the spine. Under no circumstances must the casualty be moved during this process. If in doubt, do not examine the back and assume the possibility of spinal injury; do not assume that it is muscular.

Keep the casualty still, holding the head straight. Although the casualty may be experiencing severe pain, ask them not to move, and, if possible, support their head and shoulders with clothing, blankets or other soft material, to prevent the head from moving. Ask someone to call for an ambulance and say that spinal injury is suspected.

The casualty may lose control of movement of certain limbs, sensation may be altered or abnormal, and they may have difficulty breathing. Do not move the casualty unless there is impending danger of further serious injury. If the casualty becomes unconscious and is still breathing, they should ideally be placed in the recovery position. However, depending on the severity of the back injury this may not be possible and the casualty must be monitored throughout. If the casualty is not breathing, be prepared to resuscitate.

Bleeding

There are six types of wound that cause bleeding:

(1) **Incised**. This is a clean cut with a sharp object, for example a knife. Bleeding will be profuse with this type of wound.
(2) **Lacerated**. This wound is produced by a blunt instrument which causes a torn or jagged cut. The bleeding from this type of wound will be less than that of an incised wound.
(3) **Puncture**. This could be accidental or deliberate, as in the case of a stabbing. Puncture wounds are usually deep, and the amount of bleeding depends on the severity of the wound.
(4) **Graze**. This produces minor bleeding due to a scraping or abrasion of the skin.
(5) **Contused**. This is the result of bruising and causes bleeding under the skin.
(6) **Gunshot**. This produces a small entry wound and may produce a larger exit wound.

There are three types of bleeding:
(1) **Arterial** bleeding is bright red in colour and may spurt.
(2) **Venous** bleeding is dark red in colour and tends to flow rather than spurt.
(3) **Capillary** bleeding may be bright or dark red in colour and tends to ooze.

Depending on the nature of the wound, the casualty's clothing may have to be cut to expose it. Carefully examine the wound to see if there are any foreign bodies present, and if not, cover with a dressing or the palm of the hand and apply direct pressure. If no fracture was incurred, raise the injured area. If the lower arm is involved, raise it above the casualty's heart in order to slow the supply of blood to the wound. If the leg is involved, ask the casualty to lie down, if not already doing so, and having treated the wound raise the leg slightly to slow the supply of blood to the wound.

If the bleeding is severe, the casualty may suffer from shock. It is essential that shock is recognized and treated (*see* Shock, page 35).

When dealing with wounds it is to be hoped that certain facilities will be available to assist in the first aid process: hot and cold water; soap or hand cleansers; paper towels or paper tissues designed for cleaning hands; a change of clothing for the person dealing with the casualty in case the original clothing becomes soiled; disposable gloves if the person dealing with the casualty has open wounds on the hands or the hands are dirty. Any open wound on the hands of the person dealing with the casualty should be covered with a waterproof adhesive dressing. Such precautions are essential to prevent cross infection and transmission of HIV or Hepatitis B.

If blood is flowing it cannot clot, therefore the person dealing with the casualty should observe the following guidelines:

•apply direct pressure for at least ten minutes to allow the blood to clot. If the blood is still flowing after this time, reapply pressure for at least fifteen minutes or until the ambulance arrives. If the wound is open or 'gaping', apply pressure to either side of the wound. If a sterile dressing has been applied to the wound and the blood begins to show through the dressing, apply another dressing over the original dressing. Do not remove the first dressing
•rest the casualty. This has the effect of slowing down the heart rate and thus slowing down the supply of blood to the wound, helping it to clot more readily

• if possible, elevate the wounded area. This again has the effect of reducing the amount of blood to the wound and aids clotting. Also refer to the section on Bandaging and Slings at the end of the chapter.

Broken bones

Broken bones are correctly referred to as fractures. Fractures occur either by direct or indirect impact. Direct impact means that an object, by accident or intent, has struck the bone with sufficient force to cause a fracture. An indirect fracture occurs away from the point of impact, as in a fall where the hands go forward to help stop the fall but result in fracturing of the collar bone. Fractures may be referred to as 'open' or 'closed'. An open fracture will be fairly easy to see. Invariably the bone protrudes through the skin. A closed or chipped fracture is less easy to see, especially when sprains or strains occur.

There are four main types of fracture: 'simple', 'comminuted', 'greenstick' and 'complicated'. A simple fracture is a straight break in the bone. In a comminuted fracture the bone is broken in several places. Greenstick involves a bending as well as a break and is common in children whose bones are not fully developed. A complicated fracture is one where there is an associated injury as, for example, when a fractured rib punctures a lung.

The signs and symptoms of a fracture include:

• pain and tenderness
• swelling
• loss of mobility or movement
• deformity of the injured part
• shock
• crepitus – grinding made by the broken ends of the bone that rub together.

The treatment of fractures should be carried out as follows:

• immobilize the injured area
• calm and reassure the casualty
• support the injured area
• call for an ambulance and get the casualty to hospital
• treat the casualty for shock.

In the case of a fractured skull, try to ascertain how the casualty sustained the injury. Prop the casualty up and, if available, use rolled-up clothing or blankets to support the shoulders. In most cases cerebro spinal fluid leaks from one or both ears and this takes the form of a straw-coloured liquid. Tilt the head to the affected side, where draining is taking place, and cover it with a pad. If the cerebrospinal fluid is coming from the nose, tilt the head forward.

The signs and symptoms of skull fracture include:

• pain in the form of a headache
• indentation rather than swelling – skull bones are flat and when fractured have a soft, spongy feel
• drowsiness – drifting in and out of consciousness
• unequal/unco-ordinated pupils.

Closed fractures can only be confirmed by X-ray, therefore any injury producing pain on or near the bone should be treated as a fracture.

• A fracture to the nose bone will usually incur bleeding. As with a normal nose bleed, pinch the nostrils together just below the nose bone and hold for ten minutes. Call for an ambulance and treat for shock.

• A fractured cheek bone may or may not cause bleeding but will certainly induce shock. Send for an ambulance and reassure the casualty until the ambulance arrives.
• A fractured jaw will invariably cause the jaw to drop or sag. It is important to allow the casualty to find the least painful means of supporting the jaw. Call for an ambulance. Do not bandage the jaw because the casualty could vomit, and if the jaw is bandaged or strapped they could choke.
• A fractured neck or spine should be kept as still as possible. Call for an ambulance. Comfort and reassure the casualty, and support the head and body as much as possible with rolled-up clothing or blankets. If the casualty has fallen from a height and is lying spread-eagled, assume the likelihood of a fractured spine.
• In the case of a fractured collar bone, allow the casualty to support the injured area. Call for an ambulance and treat for shock. A fracture to the lower arm or wrist may be elevated and put into a sling. With an elbow, fracture nerves can easily be damaged so the arm must remain still.
• Where there is a fracture to the ribs or sternum, call for an ambulance. Treat the casualty for shock. Because fractures to the ribs can puncture the lung, look for signs of bleeding; the casualty may cough up blood.
• If the casualty has received a fracture below the waist they will be lying on the floor. Allow the floor to support them. A fractured pelvis will be indicated by signs of uneven leg length. It is important not to move the casualty. Treat them for shock and stay with them until the ambulance arrives. The first aider should hold a casualty's fractured leg to either side of the fracture to keep the leg from moving and help prevent further damage.

Strains and sprains

Strains and sprains can sometimes resemble a fracture. A strain is damage to the muscle while a sprain is damage or injury to the ligaments attached to the joints. If in any doubt, treat the injury as a fracture, otherwise treat the casualty by employing the following principles:

• Rest.
• Ice (wrap ice before applying to the casualty).
• Compression (firm bandage).
• Elevate.

If after thirty minutes the treatment has not soothed the injury, take the casualty to hospital because the injury may well be a fracture.

Burns

In many martial arts situations there are facilities for hot drinks, or other electrical appliances such as a freezer; burns and scalds are produced by both hot and cold elements. The first aider may treat trivial burns and scalds, but if the affected area is more than one-inch square the casualty must go to hospital.

The two main risks with burns and scalds are shock and infection. Treatment should be as follows:

• cool the affected part as quickly as possible – under the tap if possible, or take the water to the casualty and immerse the affected area
• remove all constricting items if possible, for example rings and watches.
• cover the affected area with a clean, dry dressing. Do not apply antiseptic dressings, lotions, creams or grease, such as butter,

adhesive dressings, bicarb or vinegar. Do not break the skin if blisters appear.

Choking

During intervals at martial arts sessions, people may chew gum or pop a sweet in the mouth. It is undesirable to do this because if this or another foreign body lodges in the throat during training choking will occur. The casualty will certainly have difficulty breathing and consequently speaking, and if the condition persists the casualty's skin will appear to be a grey-blue colour.

Initially, bend the casualty forward and administer five sharp slaps to the back between the shoulder blades with the flat part of the hand. If the choking persists, ask the casualty to assume a standing position, stand behind them, and put your arms around their waist. As your hands meet in front of the casualty's abdomen, allow the thumb edge of one hand to rest just below the casualty's ribcage. Grasp that hand with the other hand and pull inward and upward to perform five abdominal thrusts.

If the choking still persists, alternate between back slaps and abdominal thrusts until the foreign body clears from the throat. If choking persists for any length of time the casualty may become unconscious making it necessary to resuscitate.

Convulsions

Convulsions are caused by a disturbance in the normal functioning of the brain, and result in impaired (or loss of) consciousness. Causes of convulsions may be brain damaging diseases, oxygen deprivation in the brain, head injury, and certain poisons.

Most forms of convulsion involve unconsciousness (*see* Unconsciousness, page 00). In adults the muscles throughout the body turn rigid. Breathing may be halted, but when the muscles relax the casualty usually regains consciousness. Do not apply force to restrain the casualty. If possible try to ease their fall, then try to calm and reassure them. Make the area safe by removing any objects that might cause injury to the casualty, and ask bystanders to step away from the scene. Loosen clothing and protect the casualty's head with soft material. When the convulsions cease, place the casualty in the recovery position, and stay with them until they have fully recovered.

Call for an ambulance if unconsciousness lasts for more than ten minutes, if the casualty has repeated convulsions, or if it is the casualty's first convulsion. If possible, note the time and duration of the convulsion.

In young children a fever and muscle twitching may be seen. There is holding of breath, drooling at the mouth and impaired consciousness. Remove most of their clothing and ensure a plentiful supply of fresh air. Make the area safe and support the child all round with soft padding from the head down. When the convulsions have ceased, place the child in the recovery position.

One illness associated with convulsions is epilepsy of which there are many forms. These may be split into two types: minor and major epilepsy. In minor epilepsy the casualty will look distant and stare blankly ahead. There may be twitching of the lips, eyelids, head or limbs. There may also be lip-smacking or involuntary noises. Try to get the casualty to rest in a quiet place. Make the area safe by removing obstacles that may cause injury. Be calming and reassuring and do not ask too many questions. If the casualty is unaware of what has happened, or is unaware of their condition, tell them to seek medical advice by going to the doctor.

Major epilepsy is characterized by violent seizures caused by disturbances in the activity of the brain. Although seizures can be sudden, the sufferer can sometimes show signs of an impending seizure such as an unusual taste in the mouth, or there may be a certain smell or 'aura'. When the seizure happens the casualty suddenly falls to the floor unconscious. The muscles in the body become rigid, the back arches and the breathing may stop. There is a grey-blue tinge about the lips, and congestion (an abnormal accumulation of blood) appears about the neck and face. The jaw is clenched and there may be saliva coming from the mouth. If the mouth or tongue were bitten when the jaw clenched there may be traces of blood in the saliva. There may also be a loss of bladder and bowel control.

After a few minutes the casualty's body may relax, breathing will become normal and they will regain consciousness. The casualty will almost certainly feel dazed and unaware of any action during the seizure. Severe convulsions are usually followed by a deep sleep. Place the casualty in the recovery position and monitor their pulse and breathing.

Eye injury

Naturally an injury to the eye will be painful. There may be a visible wound, a bloodshot eye, or even a foreign body lodged in the eye itself. There may also be a clear fluid from the eye injury and partial loss of vision.

Wash your hands carefully and move into a good light. Ask the casualty to lie down and place their head on your knees. Ask them to keep as still as possible and try not to use the uninjured eye to look around as this movement will affect the condition of the injured eye, particularly if there is a foreign body lodged there.

If a foreign body is present and moving then the casualty can pull the top eyelid over the bottom one to try to remove the object. Alternatively, the casualty can blink repeatedly for a moment which will hopefully dislodge the object. Blowing the nose may also help. Another option is to irrigate the eye, that is wash it with clear, cool water.

If a chemical has entered the eye in the form of a powder, brush away the majority of the powder and wash the eye with as much cool running water as possible. If possible, use a receptacle with a spout or lip to channel the water into the eye, without covering the casualty with water. If the eye has been irrigated and the foreign body is still present, the casualty must be referred to a doctor for examination.

If there is a foreign body lodged in the eye which does *not* move, do not make any attempt to move it yourself; do not irrigate, but apply a pad dressing over both eyes and send the casualty to hospital.

If no foreign body is lodged in the eye, place a sterile pad over the injured eye. Ask the casualty to keep the good eye still, or place a sterile pad over both eyes to prevent movement of the uninjured eye. If necessary, call for an ambulance or escort the casualty to hospital.

Head injury

Apart from a fractured skull, most head injuries consist of wounds. A blow to the head may result in contusion or actual bleeding. No head injury should be treated as superficial; even if the skull is not fractured there is always the possibility of internal bleeding with serious consequences. If there is bleeding, try to wear gloves to prevent cross infection. Ask the casualty to lie down, and if they become unconscious, place them in the recovery position. If the casualty is unconscious for more than three minutes, call for an ambulance and be prepared to resuscitate if required. If the wound is bleeding, apply direct pressure to it. Using a roller bandage, place the padded area over the wound and bandage firmly to slow down the flow of blood and encourage clotting. Raise the casualty's head slightly by using soft material.

Heart attack

A heart attack happens when a clot occurs in part of the heart muscle. The seriousness of the heart attack depends on the amount of the heart muscle affected: if a large part of the heart muscle is affected, the heart can stop beating, hence a heart attack or cardiac arrest; if only a small part of the heart muscle is affected the casualty may well think they have indigestion.

The signs and symptoms of a heart attack include:

• central chest pain – vice-like crushing pain
• a feeling of heaviness in the left arm
• feeling sick
• pain travelling from the neck to the left arm
• a pale, grey skin colour
• sweating profusely
• a blue tinge around the lips
• breathlessness
• fast pulse.

If you suspect that a casualty is showing the symptoms of a heart attack, call for an ambulance immediately. Explain that the casualty has severe chest pain – do not say 'heart attack' as this is very worrying for the casualty; even if they appear to be unconscious, the last sense to go is their hearing. Make the casualty as comfortable as possible in a half sitting position. Ask them to be still and to try not to move. Raise the knees and place a rolled-up coat under them for support – this helps to take some pressure off the heart. Calm and reassure the casualty, and do not leave them alone. If the heart stops, carry out resuscitation.

Angina is another very worrying condition. The casualty will usually know about this condition and will carry medication in the form of tablets or a spray. This medication acts almost immediately. Rest, calm and reassure the casualty, and if the pain does not go away call for an ambulance.

A **stroke** is an interruption of the blood supply to the brain, for example when a clot blocks a major blood vessel in the brain. The severity of the stroke depends on the amount of damage caused by the blockage of the blood vessel; some strokes could be minor, others major.

When a stroke affects the right side of the brain, the left side of the body is affected. Conversely, the right side of the body is affected when the left side of the brain is affected. The casualty may slump to the floor, and may have already experienced headaches and slurring of speech. Call for an ambulance. Leave the casualty in the position into which they have slumped, and observe and reassure. If the casualty becomes unconscious, place in the recovery position. Do not administer anything by mouth – whatever is given may well hinder

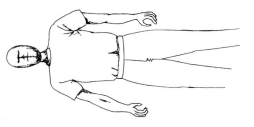

Fig 1

Fig 3

the progress of the paramedics or hospital staff. Treat the casualty for shock.

Resuscitation (Adult)

Assess the casualty. Check for a response by tapping them firmly on the shoulders and saying loudly: 'What has happened? Open your eyes.' If the casualty comes around, place them in the recovery position and monitor their progress. If the casualty does not come around, check again for a response by either pinching the back of their hand or rubbing your knuckles firmly

Fig 2

up and down their sternum. If there is still no response, clear the airway by checking the mouth to see if there are any obstructions such as foreign bodies. Check for a pulse. Place one hand on the forehead and two fingers under the chin and tilt the head backward.

When someone is unconscious they lose their survival reflexes and the tongue can lodge at the back of the throat preventing breathing. Because the tongue is attached to the jaw with muscle, tilting the head back pulls the tongue forward and clears the airway.

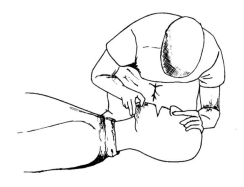

Fig 4

Check the casualty's breathing for at least ten seconds by putting your cheek close to their mouth. Try to feel the casualty's breath on your cheek, and look at the chest to see if there is breathing movement, that is rising and falling of the chest.

If the casualty is not breathing, call for an ambulance and give two ventilations: pinch the casualty's nose closed and blow into their mouth. After each ventilation look at the chest to see if the ventilation was successful. If it was successful you will see

Fig 5

Fig 6

Fig 7

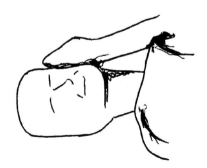

Fig 8

the casualty's chest deflating. Feel for a pulse. If the casualty has a pulse but is still not breathing, give ten ventilations with a slight pause between each.

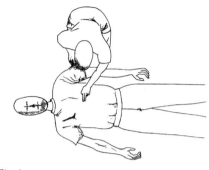

Fig 9

If the casualty starts breathing, place them in the recovery position.

If the casualty does not start breathing and there is no longer a pulse, begin resuscitation.

First find the base of the casualty's sternum by following the line of the bottom ribs to the centre of the chest. At this point place two fingers at the base of the breastbone and slide the heel of the palm of the

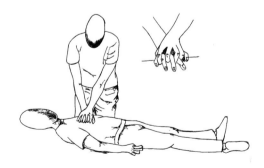

Fig 10

Fig 11

other hand down from the top of the breastbone to the two fingers.

Keep that hand where it is and place the other hand on top, interlocking the fingers and pulling them slightly upward.

In a kneeling position, with the knees slightly apart, straighten the arms and move the body weight over the casualty. Using the body weight, press down on to the casualty's sternum to a depth of about 5cm (2in) ten times, then give two more ventilations. These are referred to as 'chest compressions'. Try to regulate the compressions to the normal rate of the heart beat, about 60–80 beats per minute. Check the pulse and the breathing. If neither are present continue resuscitation – two ventilations followed by ten chest compressions. *Never assume that a casualty will not recover.* Against all odds continue resuscitation until the ambulance arrives.

If you are alone with the casualty, assess whether unconsciousness is due to injury or drowning if close to water. Check the danger both to the casualty and to yourself – you will be of little help if you fall down and break a leg, for example. Check the casualty for a response. Check the airway and their breathing. If the casualty is not breathing, give two ventilations and check the pulse. If the casualty has a pulse give ten

further ventilations, then go for help. If the casualty does not have a pulse, give one minute of resuscitation then go for help. Come back and once again check the danger, response, airway and breathing.

Shock

Many people are confused about what shock is; they think that emotional or mental trauma is shock, and while this is true, in this instance we are concerned with medical shock. Medical shock is a sudden problem with the circulatory system caused by a reduction in body fluids. The most common cause of shock is a heart attack. Shock also occurs when the flow of blood around the body is reduced either by external or internal bleeding. Other causes of shock can be diarrhoea, vomiting, burns and electric shock. The reason for this is that the body responds to the sudden loss of fluids by withdrawing the blood supply from the surface of the body to cater for major organs at the core of the body, such as the heart and kidneys. When this happens adrenaline is pumped into the body.

Shock is recognizable by certain characteristics:

• a rapid pulse
• pale grey skin, especially inside the lips – a fingernail or ear lobe will not regain its colour when pressed
• cold, clammy skin and sweating
• possible cyanosis – a blue tinge around the lips and fingertips.

As shock develops other characteristics begin to show:

• giddiness and weakness
• nausea and possibly vomiting

• thirst
• rapid, shallow breathing
• a fast, irregular pulse.

As the oxygen supply to the brain is depleting, the casualty may:

• become restless, anxious or aggressive
• gasp for air by yawning (referred to as 'air hunger')
• become unconscious.

Eventually the heart will stop beating.

When treating a casualty for shock, ask someone to call for an ambulance and instruct them to come back and tell you that they have done so. Try to ascertain why shock was incurred. For example, severe external bleeding may be the cause, in which case treat the bleeding first to reduce the loss of body fluid. Lay the casualty down. Try to keep the head low, and, if no broken bones are present, raise and support the casualty's legs – this will help the blood flow to the major organs. Loosen any tight clothing such as neck ties and belts. Keep the casualty warm but *do not use artificial heat;* use a blanket or extra clothing to help the body regain its normal temperature naturally. Do not allow the casualty to move or take anything by mouth, even a cigarette. If the casualty complains of thirst, moisten the lips only. Monitor the casualty and be prepared to perform resuscitation if necessary.

Electric Shock

Shock can be caused by electric shock from low-voltage appliances such as electric kettles, drills and so on, or high-voltage systems such as overhead power lines. Electricity passes a current through the body which can stun a casualty, stop their breathing or even stop the heart beating. Burns may appear at the point of entry and the point of exit.

Contact with high-voltage electricity is usually fatal. It can 'arc' up to 18m (20yds) and the usual protection such as dry wood or clothing will not prevent the current from passing from the casualty to yourself. The casualty must not be approached until the power is cut off and isolated. In the event of high-voltage electrical shock, call the emergency services. Once the power has been isolated, approach the casualty. The casualty will certainly be unconscious, so follow the procedure for unconsciousness and be prepared to carry out resuscitation.

When approaching a casualty who has suffered a low-voltage shock, first of all break the contact by switching off the power at the mains; remove the plug, or use a piece of wood or some other non-conductive material, such as wood, a telephone directory, a rubber or plastic mat or a thick layer of newspaper, to separate the casualty from the source of the power. *Do not touch the casualty's flesh with any part of your body.* When the casualty is free from the source of the power, check their breathing and pulse and be prepared to carry out resuscitation if necessary. Cool any burns with lots of cold water, and place the casualty in the recovery position. Call for an ambulance.

Lightning is also a cause of shock: it can set your clothes on fire and can be fatal. Get the casualty and yourself away from the place where the lightning struck. Check their breathing and pulse and be prepared to carry out resuscitation if necessary. Place the casualty in the recovery position.

Another form of shock is anaphylactic shock. This is a massive allergic reaction which is very serious and can be fatal. It is possible for the condition to develop within seconds or minutes after an injection of a particular drug, an insect sting, or the ingestion of certain types of food. The condition causes substances in the blood to dilate the blood vessels and constrict the airway. Because of this the blood pressure drops and there is difficulty in breathing. Call for an ambulance.

The signs of anaphylactic shock include:

• anxiety
• red and blotchy skin
• swelling of the face and neck
• eyes may become puffy
• breathing problems – tight chest, wheezing and 'air hunger'
• rapid pulse.

The casualty needs oxygen and an injection of adrenaline. Help them to sit in a position that will assist their breathing. If the casualty becomes unconscious, place them in the recovery position. Keep them warm and be prepared to perform resuscitation if necessary.

Unconsciousness

Unconsciousness is the loss of survival reflexes. There are a range of causes, such as fainting, infantile convulsions, shock, electric shock, hypothermia, heart attack, stroke, head injury, asphyxia, poisoning, epilepsy and diabetes. Levels of consciousness are defined as **alert** – responding to normal conversation; **responds to voice** – unable to talk, open eyes but responds to the sound of your voice; **reacts to pain** – flinches when the hand is pinched for example; and **unconscious**.

The main danger of unconsciousness is choking, because the tongue may lodge in the throat, false teeth may fall to the back of the mouth, or foreign bodies may lodge in the throat. If a casualty becomes unconscious, follow the procedure for resuscitation.

Bandaging and slings

The first aid outlined in this section is meant as a guide. There is no substitute for qualified tuition from organizations such St John Ambulance or Colleges of Further and Higher Education, who work in conjunction with the major teaching bodies on first aid.

There are many ways of using bandages, and to some extent it is an art acquired through practise. Consequently, descriptions prove to have limited use. Applying a bandage may appear to be a simple matter, but requires hands-on experience with a qualified professional. A bandage which is applied too loosely will be ineffective and one applied too tightly will restrict blood flow and cause other problems. The descriptions here, therefore, are simplified and reduced to the most common forms of use.

Basically, there are three types of bandaging: *roller*, *tubular* and *triangular*. A roller bandage can be made of cotton, gauze or linen, and is applied by wrapping around the wound in a spiral fashion. Roller bandages may be *open-weave*, *conforming* or *crepe*.

Open-weave are used to hold light dressings in place and allow good ventilation. They are unsuitable for wounds requiring pressure or joints that need support. As their name suggests, conforming bandages mould to the shape of the body and may be used to secure dressings and support injuries. Because of their flexibility, crepe bandages are used to give support around joints.

Tubular bandages are made of gauze and are commonly used on elbows, ankles, fingers and toes. They are good for holding light dressings in place, but because of their loose fitting are inadequate for controlling bleeding wounds.

Triangular bandages have several uses. They can be used to secure bulky dressings and splints; to immobilize injured feet and ankles; or to hold a scalp dressing in place. They are commonly used to support arms in the form of a sling.

Because of the complexity of bandaging and dressing and the inability to illustrate adequately such applications, I feel there is little need to expand this section. Seek professional advice. If you are unsure about any of the procedures, leave bandaging and dressing to the ambulance crew or paramedics. Lack of knowledge and experience can lead to more harm than good, not to mention the responsibility to you should anything adversely affect the wound or injury as a result of your actions.

7 Additional Kata

In Funakoshi's book, *Karate-Do Kyohan*, there are eighteen kata listed, from *Taikyoku Shodan* to *Gankaku*. In the majority of cases clubs use these kata to form the curriculum for students working through the ranks from white belt to black. There are, however, many more kata which are less well known. The following twelve kata are usually practised and taught by more advanced

karateka. These kata are: *Sochin, Meikyo Dai, Bassai Sho, Kanku Sho, Nijushiho, Jin, Wankan, Chinte, Unsu, Goju Shi Ho Dai, Goju Shi Ho Sho,* and *Meikyo Sho*. Other kata exist for those who wish to search for them.

The intention of this section is to describe these additional kata. To learn kata properly one needs a good teacher; however, the descriptions found in this book form a reference to the moves and techniques which are virtually impossible to remember in relatively short lessons. Interpretation and *Bunkai* can only be pursued when the pattern of the kata is thoroughly mastered. Learning the kata in class and then referring to this book will greatly enhance the students' ability to progress. This is particularly significant as most people have busy lifestyles which leave limited time and mental capacity to acquire a skill as profound as karate-do. 'Little and often' is a good maxim for learning karate-do, and we all have gaps in our daily lives which can be constructively filled by reference to books.

Japanese terms are used in the kata descriptions, explanations of which are provided at the back of the book with photographic illustrations.

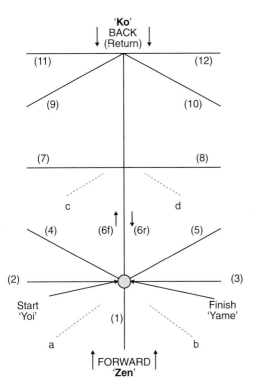

Fig 12 Direction lines used in Kata Enbusen.

SOCHIN

Step forward with the right foot, line 6f, into a straddle stance (*Sochin Dachi*). Raise the left arm to a high-level blocking posi-

39

tion, and move the right arm to a low-level blocking position (*Muso Gamae*). Step with the left foot, line 6f, into a straddle stance (*Sochin Dachi*). Crossing the arms at the chest, draw the right open hand under the left upper arm, outward to the left and forward in an arc (*Migi Chudan Tate Shuto Uke*). Drawing the right fist to the right hip, thrust forward with the left fist (*Hidari Chudan Zuki*), then, drawing the left fist to the left hip, thrust forward with the right fist (*Migi Chudan Gyaku Zuki*). Turn 90 degrees anti-clockwise, line 2 (*Kokutsu Dachi*). Raise the right arm to a high-level blocking position and move the left arm to a low-level blocking position (*Manji Gamae*).

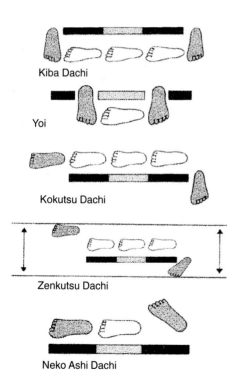

Fig 13 Stance foot positions.

Kiba Dachi

Yoi

Kokutsu Dachi

Zenkutsu Dachi

Neko Ashi Dachi

Step with the right foot, line 2, into a straddle stance (*Sochin Dachi*). Raise the left arm to a high-level blocking position, and move the right arm to a low-level blocking position (*Muso Gamae*). Step with the left foot, line 2. Allow the arms to cross at the chest, and draw the right open hand under the left upper arm, outward to the left and forward in an arc (*Migi Chudan Tate Shuto Uke*). Drawing the right fist to the right hip, drive forward with the left fist (*Hidari Chudan Zuki*), then, drawing the left fist to the left hip, thrust forward with the right fist (*Migi Chudan Gyaku Zuki*).

Step backward with the left foot, and turn anti-clockwise to face line 3. Raise the right arm to a high-level blocking position, and move the left arm to a low-level blocking position (*Manji Gamae*). Step with the right foot, line 3, into a straddle stance (*Sochin Dachi*). Raise the left arm to a high-level blocking position and move the right arm to a low-level blocking position (*Muso Gamae*). Step with the left foot, line 3, into a straddle stance (*Sochin Dachi*). Crossing the arms at the chest, draw the right open hand under the left upper arm, outward to the left and forward in an arc (*Migi Chudan Tate Shuto Uke*). Drawing the right fist to the right hip, thrust forward in an arc with the left back fist (*Hidari Chudan Zuki*), then, drawing the left fist to the left hip, thrust forward with the right fist (*Migi Chudan Gyaku Zuki*). Drawing the left foot back, turn to face line 2. Drive outward with a left fist and a left foot middle-level strike (*Hidari Yoko Geri Keage – Hidari Uraken Zuki*).

Lower the left foot, line 2, into a straddle stance (*Sochin Dachi*), and drive around in an arc with the right elbow to strike the left open hand (*Migi Enpi Uchi*). Turn 180 degrees clockwise, line 3. Drive outward with a right fist and a right foot middle-level strike (*Migi Yoko Geri Keage – Migi Uraken Zuki*). Lower the right foot, line 3, into a straddle stance (*Sochin Dachi*), and drive around in an arc with the left elbow to strike the right open hand (*Migi Enpi Uke*).

Stepping backward with the right foot, turn clockwise to face line 2 (*Kokutsu Dachi – Migi Chudan Shuto Uke*). Step diagonally with the left foot, line a (*Kokutsu Dachi – Hidari Chudan Shuto Uke*). Stepping across with the left foot, turn to face line 3 (*Kokutsu Dachi – Hidari Chudan Shuto Uke*). Step diagonally with the right foot, line b (*Kokutsu Dachi – Migi Chudan Shuto Uke*). Step with the right foot, line 1 (*Kokutsu Dachi – Migi Chudan Shuto Uke*). Step with the left foot, line 1 (*Kokutsu Dachi – Hidari Chudan Shuto Uke*). Press down with the left open palm (*Hidari Osae Uke*), then, moving the body weight forward, change to a front stance (*Zenkutsu Dachi*), and drive forward with a right four-finger spear hand (*Migi Nukite*).

Draw the right foot toward the left foot, then raise the left knee to make a forward kick (*Hidari Mae Geri*). Immediately follow this action with a right front kick (*Migi Mae Geri*), then, drawing the right fist past the right temple, drive forward with a right back fist strike (*Nagashi Uke – Uraken Uchi*). Turning 180 degrees anti-clockwise, execute a right crescent moon kick (*Mikazuki Geri*), and step into a straddle stance (*Sochin Dachi*). At the same time, raise the left arm to a high-level blocking position and move the right arm to a low-level blocking position (*Muso Gamae*).

Step diagonally with the left foot, line 4, into a straddle stance (*Sochin Dachi*), and, drawing the right fist to the right hip, execute a left middle-level block (*Hidari Chudan Uchi Uke*). Step with the right foot, line 4, into a straddle stance (*Sochin Dachi*), and, drawing the left fist to the left hip, execute a right middle-level punch (*Migi Chudan Zuki*). Step with the right foot, line 5, into a straddle stance (*Sochin Dachi*), and, drawing the left fist to the left hip, execute a right middle-level block (*Migi Chudan Uchi Uke*). Step with the left foot, line 5, into a straddle stance (*Sochin Dachi*) and, drawing the right fist to the right hip, execute a left middle-level punch (*Hidari Chudan Zuki*).

Stepping across with the left foot, line 6f, into a straddle stance (*Sochin Dachi*), execute a left middle-level block (*Hidari Chudan Uchi Uke*). Follow this immediately by twisting at the waist (*Hanmi*), allowing the arms to cross at the chest, then, while drawing the left fist to the left hip, execute a right reverse middle-level block (*Migi Chudan Gyaku Uchi Uke*).

Driving with the right foot forward, line 6f, execute a high-level front kick (*Migi Jodan Mae Geri*), then step back with the right foot, line 6r, into a straddle stance (*Sochin Dachi*). Follow this immediately by driving the left fist forward with a middle-level strike, while drawing the right fist to the right nipple (*Hidari Yumi Zuki*). Without pausing, draw the left fist to the left hip and drive forward with a right middle-level punch (*Migi Chudan Gyaku Zuki*). Return to *Yoi*.

MEIKYO DAI

Step with the right foot, line 3, into a horse riding stance (*Kiba Dachi*), and draw the fists to the hips (*Ryo Goshi Gamae*). Open the hands and drive them forward and upward to about chest height (*Joshin Gamae*). Step with the left foot, line 4, into a front stance (*Zenkutsu Dachi*), and execute a left low-level block (*Hidari Gedan Barai*). Step with the right foot, line 4, into a front stance (*Zenkutsu Dachi*), and execute a right middle-level punch (*Migi Chudan Oi Zuki*). Step across with the right foot, line 5, into a front stance (*Zenkutsu Dachi*), and execute a right low-level block (*Migi Gedan Barai*). Step with the left foot, line 5, into a front stance (*Zenkutsu Dachi*), and execute a left middle-level punch (*Hidari Chudan Oi Zuki*). Step across with the left foot, line 6f, into a back stance (*Kokutsu Dachi*), and drive the left open hand to a low-level position and the right open hand to a high-level position and execute a Jo Staff block (*Morote Jo Uke*). Step forward with the right foot into a front stance (*Zenkutsu Dachi*), and, exchanging the position of the hands, execute a *Jo Kuzami*. Follow this immediately by making a short sliding movement (*Yori Ashi*) and executing a right middle-level punch (*Migi Oi Zuki*).

Turn anti-clockwise to face line 6r, stepping with the right foot, line 11, into a horse riding stance and draw the fists to the hips (*Ryo Goshi Gamae*). Open the hands and drive them forward and upward to about chest height (*Joshin Gamae*). Step with the left foot, line 10, into a front stance (*Zenkutsu Dachi*), and execute a left middle-level block (*Hidari Chudan Uchi Uke*). Step with the right foot, line 10, into a front stance (*Zenkutsu Dachi*), and execute a right middle-level punch (*Migi Chudan Oi Zuki*). Step across with the right foot, line 9, into a front stance (*Zenkutsu Dachi*), and execute a right middle-level block (*Migi Chudan Uchi Uke*). Step with the left foot, line 9, into a front stance (*Zenkutsu Dachi*), and execute a left middle-level punch (*Hidari Chudan Oi Zuki*).

Step across with the left foot, line 6r, into a back stance (*Kokutsu Dachi*), and drive the left open hand to a low-level position and the right open hand to a high-level position and execute a Jo Staff block (*Morote Jo Uke*). Step forward with the right foot into a front stance (*Zenkutsu Dachi*), and, exchanging the position of the hands, execute a *Jo Kuzami*. Immediately follow this by making a short sliding movement (*Yori Ashi*) and executing a right middle-level punch (*Migi Oi Zuki*).

Turn anti-clockwise to face line 6f, stepping with the right foot, line 3, into a horse riding stance (*Kiba Dachi*), and draw the fists to the hips (*Ryo Goshi Gamae*). Open the hands and drive them forward and upward to about chest height (*Joshin Gamae*). Step with the left foot, line 4, into a front stance (*Zenkutsu Dachi*), and execute a left high-level block (*Hidari Jodan Age Uke*). Step with the right foot, line 4, into a front stance (*Zenkutsu Dachi*), and execute a right middle-level punch (*Migi Chudan Oi Zuki*). Step across with the right foot, line 5, into a front stance (*Zenkutsu Dachi*), and execute a right high-level block (*Migi Jodan Age Uke*). Step with the left foot, line 5, into a front stance (*Zenkutsu Dachi*), and execute a left middle-level punch (*Hidari Chudan Oi Zuki*). Step across with the left foot, line 6f, into a horse riding stance (*Kiba Dachi*). The body is facing in the direction of line 8, and the head directed along line 6f. Drawing the right fist to the right hip, execute a left middle-level hammer fist strike (*Hidari Chudan Tettsui Uchi*). Drive around with the right foot with a crescent moon kick (*Migi Mikazuki Geri*), strike the left open hand, draw the right foot back to the horse riding stance (*Kiba Dachi*), and lower the arms out to the sides of the body (*Ryowan*

Gamae). Facing line 6f, change the stance to a back stance (*Kiba Dachi*), and raise the left arm to a high-level blocking position and the right also to a high-level blocking position (*Morote Haiwan Uke*).

Step forward with the right foot, line 6f, into a back stance (*Kokutsu Dachi*), and exchange the positions of the arms (*Morote Haiwan Uke*). Step forward with the left foot into a front stance (*Zenkutsu Dachi*), and rotate the arm in the opposite direction in front of the body and out to the sides of the body (*Ryowan Gamae*).

Step forward with the right foot, line 6f, into a back stance (*Kokutsu Dachi*), and raise both arms in front of the body to about chest height (*Ryowan Uchi Uke*), then, pushing forward with the right foot into a front stance (*Zenkutsu Dachi*), execute a right middle-level punch (*Migi Chudan Zuki*). Maintaining the front stance, twist the body anti-clockwise towards line 6r, and draw the left hand around to the rear to a high-level open hand blocking position (*Hidari Jodan Age Zuki*). Pushing backward and driving from the left foot, leap high into the air (*Sankaku Tobi*), and, while turning, strike the left open hand with the right elbow (*Migi Enpi Uchi*).

After the leap, drop into a back stance (*Kokutsu Dachi*) with the right foot forward, and execute a right middle-level knife hand block (*Migi Chudan Shuto Uke*). Step back with the left foot, line 6r, into a back stance (*Kokutsu Dachi*), and execute a left middle-level knife hand block (*Hidari Chudan Shuto Uke*). Draw the right foot to the left foot and return to *Yoi*.

BASSAI SHO

Step forward with the right foot, line 6f, into a crossed stance (*Kosa Dachi*). Raise the open hands to a high level, with the back of the left hand resting against the palm of the right hand (*Haishu Awaze Uke*). Turn 180 degrees anti-clockwise while stepping backward with the left foot, line 6r, into a back stance (*Kokutsu Dachi*). At the same time, extend the left open hand to a middle-level blocking position and the right open hand to a high-level blocking position as if blocking against a Bo Staff (*Morote Koko Uke*). While raising the left hand to a high-level position, allow the right hand to turn clockwise until the palm is facing downward (*Soihei Bo Dori*).

Make a three-quarter turn clockwise to face line 3, drawing the left foot around to the right foot into an informal attention stance (*Heisoku Dachi*). At the same time, sweep the right open hand around in front of the body in an anti-clockwise direction to perform a low-level block (*Haito Sukui Nage*). Follow this with a large anti-clockwise circle with the right hand. At the end of the circle, close the fist to make a low-level hammer fist strike (*Gedan Tettsui Uke*).

Step with the left foot, line 3, into a back stance (*Kokutsu Dachi*). At the same time, extend the left open hand to a middle-level blocking position and the right open hand to a high-level blocking position as if blocking against a Bo Staff (*Morote Koko Uke*). While raising the left hand to a high-level position, allow the right hand to turn clockwise until the palm is facing downward (*Soihei Bo Dori*).

Turn the body to face line 6f, but look toward line 3. Draw the right foot to the left foot into an informal attention stance, and the open hands to the left side of the body (*Haito Koshi Gamae*).

Execute a right middle-level side kick (*Yoko Geri Keage*), and at the same time, execute a right open hand high-level block

(*Doji Haito Uchi*). Lower the right foot into a horse riding stance (*Kiba Dachi*) along line 3. Drive the left open hand around to the right and forward (*Hidari Tate Shuto Uke*). Execute a right middle-level punch (*Migi Chudan Zuki*), followed by a left middle-level punch (*Hidari Chudan Zuki*). Look toward line 2 and change the stance to a back stance (*Kokutsu Dachi*). Raise the right arm out to the right side of the body in an 'L' shape to high level, and move the left arm down to a low-level blocking position (*Manji Gamae*). Pivoting on the heels, turn to face line 3 in a back stance (*Kokutsu Dachi*). Raise the left arm out to the left side of the body in an 'L' shape to high level, and move the right arm down to a low-level blocking position (*Manji Gamae*).

Draw the left foot toward the right foot, then step with the right foot, line 6f, into a back stance (*Kokutsu Dachi*), and execute a right middle-level knife hand block (*Migi Shuto Uke*). Step with the left foot, line 6f, into a back stance (*Kokutsu Dachi*), and execute a left middle-level knife hand block (*Migi Shuto Uke*). Step with the right foot, line 6f, into a back stance (*Kokutsu Dachi*), and execute a right middle-level knife hand block (*Migi Shuto Uke*). Step backward with the right foot, line 6r, into a back stance (*Kokutsu Dachi*), and execute a left middle-level knife hand block (*Migi Shuto Uke*). Changing to a front stance, allow the body to twist slightly to the left. Sweep the right hand around and in front of the body to about shoulder height, and bring the left hand to rest on the back of the right wrist. Pull both hands downward to about middle level (*Kaeshi Dori*), and, raising the right knee, stamp down to low level with the heel of the right foot (*Gedan Kesage*). Then, pivoting on the left foot, turn 180 degrees to face line 6r, step backward into a back

stance (*Kokutsu Dachi*), and drive both arms forward to perform two middle-level forearm blocking actions (*Ryowan Uchi Uke*). Drive quickly up and down with the fists as if having made two short rising fist strikes (*Heiko Ura Zuki*). Sweep forward with the right foot, line 6r (*Migi Ashi Barai*), and step along line 6r into a horse riding stance (*Kiba Dachi*). Sweep around with the right forearm (*Doji Uke*), and drive both fists out to the right side of the body (*Morote Zuki*). Turn 180 degrees anti-clockwise to face line 6f, and assume a front stance (*Zenkutsu Dachi*). Execute a left low-level block (*Hidari Gedan Barai*), then step forward with the right foot, line 6f, into a front stance (*Zenkutsu Dachi*), and execute a right middle-level punch (*Migi Chudan Zuki*).

Turn 180 degrees anti-clockwise to face line 6r, and bring the outer edges of both hands together at about chest height, then, moving along line 6r, sweep around with the right foot (*Migi Ashi Barai*), and drive both fists out to the right side of the body (*Morote Zuki*). Sweep around with the left foot (*Hidari Ashi Barai*), and drive both fists out to the left side of the body (*Morote Zuki*). Sweep around with the right foot (*Migi Ashi Barai*), and drive both fists out to the right side of the body (*Morote Zuki*).

Step across with the left foot to line 2. Lean forward until the head is level with the right knee. Turn the head and upper body to look towards line 2. Sweep the left open hand in a forward arc out to the rear of the body, until it is in line with the left foot and above head height. At the same time, draw the right hand toward the left shoulder until the thumb edge is almost touching the left shoulder. Draw the hands down toward the lower abdomen (*Jodan Shuto Doji Uke*), and sweep the left foot toward the right foot (*Ura*

Ashigake) into a cat stance (*Neko Ashi Dachi*). Step with the left foot over the right foot, then drive backward with the right heel along line 3. Lean forward until the head is level with the left knee. Turn the head and upper body to look towards line 3. Sweep the right open hand in a forward arc out to the rear of the body, until it is in line with the left foot and above head height. At the same time, draw the left hand toward the left shoulder until the thumb edge is almost touching the right shoulder. Draw the hands down toward the lower abdomen (*Jodan Shuto Doji Uke*), and sweep the right foot toward the left foot (*Ura Ashigake*) into a cat stance (*Neko Ashi Dachi*). Return to *Yoi*.

KANKU SHO

Step with the left foot, line 2, into a back stance (*Kokutsu Dachi*), and, looking toward line 3, execute a right augmented middle-level block (*Migi Chudan Morote Uke*). Transfer the body weight to the right foot, and, pivoting on the heels, turn to look along line 2. Assume a back stance (*Kokutsu Dachi*), and execute a left augmented middle-level block (*Hidari Chudan Morote Uke*). Step back with the right foot, line 1, and look toward line 6f. Assume a back stance (*Kokutsu Dachi*), and execute a left augmented middle-level block (*Hidari Chudan Morote Uke*). Step forward with the right foot, line 6f, into a front stance (*Zenkutsu Dachi*), and, at the same time, execute a right middle-level punch (*Migi Chudan Oi Zuki*). Follow this by pivoting the right arm in a clockwise direction to perform a middle-level block (*Hineri Kaeshi*).

Step forward with the left foot, line 6f, into a front stance (*Zenkutsu Dachi*), and, at the same time, execute a left middle-level punch (*Hidari Chudan Oi Zuki*). Follow this by pivoting the left arm in an anti-clockwise direction to perform a middle-level block (*Hineri Kaeshi*). Step forward with the right foot, line 6f, into a front stance (*Zenkutsu Dachi*), and, at the same time, execute a right middle-level punch (*Migi Chudan Oi Zuki*).

Turn 180 degrees to line 6r and assume a half facing stance (*Moto Dachi*). At the same time, sweep the right hand around and in front of the body to about shoulder height, and bring the left hand to rest on the back of the right wrist (*Soete Kake Dori*). Pull both hands downward to about middle level (*Tsukami Dori*), and execute a right front kick (*Migi Chudan Mae Geri*). Follow this with a left palm middle-level block (*Hidari Chudan Hirate Osae Uke*). Draw the left foot to the outside edge of the right foot into a crossed stance (*Kosa Dachi*), and while drawing the left fist to the left hip, drive downward from high level with the back of the right fist to about head height (*Migi Tate Uraken Uchi*). Step back with the left foot, line 6f, into a front stance (*Zenkutsu Dachi*), and execute a right middle-level block (*Migi Chudan Uchi Uke*), followed by a left middle-level punch (*Hidari Chudan Gyaku Zuki*), and a right middle-level punch (*Migi Chudan Zuki*).

Turn 180 degrees anti-clockwise to face line 6f, and assume a back stance (*Kokutsu Dachi*). Draw the right arm toward the right side of the body into a middle-level blocking position, and the left arm downward into a low-level blocking position (*Kasui Ken*). Draw the left foot slightly to the right foot into a natural posture (*Shizentai*), and bring the right fist to rest at the right hip while performing a left low-level block (*Gedan Gamae*). Sliding the left foot forward, line 6f, step into a front stance (*Zenkutsu Dachi*), sweep the right hand around and in front of the body to about shoulder height, and bring the left hand to rest on the back of the right wrist (*Soete Kake Dori*). Pull both hands downward to about middle level (*Tsukami Dori*), and execute a right front kick (*Migi Chudan Mae Geri*). Follow this with a left palm middle-level block (*Hidari Chudan Hirate Osae Uke*). Draw the left foot to the outside edge of the right foot into a crossed stance (*Kosa Dachi*), and while drawing the left fist to the left hip, drive downward from high level with the back of the right fist to about head height (*Migi Tate Uraken Uchi*). Step back with the left foot, line 6r, into a front stance (*Zenkutsu Dachi*), and execute a right middle-level block (*Migi Chudan Uchi Uke*), followed by a left middle-level punch (*Hidari Chudan Gyaku Zuki*), and a right middle-level punch (*Migi Chudan Zuki*).

Turn 180 degrees anti-clockwise to face line 6r, and assume a back stance (*Kokutsu Dachi*). Draw the right arm toward the right side of the body into a middle-level blocking position, and move the left arm downward into a low-level blocking position (*Kasui Ken*). Draw the left foot slightly to the right foot into a natural posture (*Shizentai*), and bring the right fist to rest at the right hip while performing a left low-level block (*Gedan Gamae*).

Step with the left foot, line 8, while raising the right arm to the right side of the body in an upper level block, an 'L' shape, and moving the left arm downward to a low-level block (*Manji Uke*). Slide along line 8 slightly (*Yori Ashi*), into a horse riding stance (*Kiba Dachi*), and drive to the left of the body with both fists: the left arm should be fully extended and the right fist should be level with, and about 4in away

from the left nipple (*Sokumen Morote Zuki*). Step with the right foot, line 7, while raising the left arm to the left side of the body in an upper level block, an 'L' shape, and moving the right arm downward to a low-level block (*Manji Uke*). Slide along line 7 slightly (*Yori Ashi*), into a horse riding stance (*Kiba Dachi*), and drive to the right of the body with both fists: the right arm should be fully extended and the left fist should be level with, and about 4in away from the right nipple (*Sokumen Morote Zuki*).

Step with the right foot, line 6r, into a back stance (*Kokutsu Dachi*). Drive the right open hand forward to a point about 6in above and in front of the right knee, and, at the same time, drive the left hand forward and upward to a point about 6in above and in front of the head (*Bo Uke*). Slide forward with the right foot (*Yori Ashi*), and drive forward with the right hand while drawing the left hand down toward the abdomen (*Bo Dori Tsuki Otoshi*).

Turn 180 degrees to change position and leap into the air, and while leaping turn another 180 degrees to complete a 360-degree turn (*Tenshin Tobi Gaeshi*); land with the right foot forward in a back stance (*Kokutsu Dachi*), and execute a right middle-level knife hand block (*Migi Chudan Shuto Uke*). Looking along line 8, draw the left foot toward the right knee. Execute a left rising side kick and a simultaneous left back fist strike along line 8 (*Hidari Yoko Geri Keage – Hidari Uraken Uchi*). Follow this by stepping with the left foot, line 8, into a front stance and striking the left open palm with the right elbow (*Migi Mae Enpi*). Looking along line 7, draw the right foot toward the left knee. Execute a right rising side kick and a simultaneous right back fist strike along line 7 (*Migi Yoko Geri Keage – Migi Uraken Uchi*). Follow this by stepping with the right foot, line 7, into a front stance and striking the right open palm with the left elbow (*Hidari Mae Enpi*).

Turn the body to face line 6r, and assume a half facing stance (*Moto Dachi*). At the same time, sweep the right hand around and in front of the body to about shoulder height, and bring the left hand to rest on the back of the right wrist (*Soete Kake Dori*). Pull both hands downward to about middle level (*Tsukami Dori*), and execute a right front kick (*Migi Chudan Mae Geri*). Follow this with a left palm middle-level block (*Hidari Chudan Hirate Osae Uke*). Draw the left foot to the outside edge of the right foot into a crossed stance (*Kosa Dachi*), and while drawing the left fist to the left hip, drive downward from high level with the back of the right fist to about head height (*Migi Tate Uraken Uchi*).

Step back with the left foot, line 6f, into a front stance (*Zenkutsu Dachi*), and execute a right middle-level block (*Migi Chudan Uchi Uke*), followed by a left middle-level punch (*Hidari Chudan Gyaku Zuki*), and a right middle-level punch (*Migi Chudan Zuki*). While maintaining the front stance, drive the back of the left open hand out toward the left of the body and high toward the rear (*Haishu Uke*). Transfer the body weight to the left leg and, leaping high into the air and turning 360 degrees, sweep across with the right foot at head height (*Jodan Tobi Ashi Barai*), then drive out, line 6f, with the right heel (*Tobi Ushiro Geri*), and land in a deep front stance with the chest over the right thigh and the palms of the hands flat on the floor either side of the right foot (*Ryote Fuse*). Step with the left foot, line 6r, as slowly as possible into a back stance (*Kokutsu Dachi*), and execute a low-level open hands block (*Morote Gedan Shuto Uke*).

Step with the right foot, line 6r, into a back stance (*Kokutsu Dachi*), and execute a right middle-level knife hand block (*Migi Chudan Shuto Uke*). Make a three-quarter turn anti-clockwise and step with the left foot, line 2, into a front stance (*Zenkutsu Dachi*), and execute a left middle-level forearm block (*Hidari Uchi Uke*). Step with the right foot, line 2, and execute a right middle-level punch (*Migi Chudan Oi Zuki*). Turn 180 degrees clockwise and step with the right foot, line 3, into a front stance (*Zenkutsu Dachi*), and execute a right middle-level forearm block (*Migi Uchi Uke*). Step with the left foot, line 2, and execute a left middle-level punch (*Hidari Chudan Oi Zuki*). Return to *Yoi*.

NIJUSHIHO

Step back with the right foot, line 1, into a back stance (*Kokutsu Dachi*). At the same time, raise both open hands high and to the front to just above head height, then draw them downward (*Ryusui No Kamae*). Slide forward a little, line 6f (*Yori Ashi*), and, driving the right fist under the left arm, execute a middle-level punch (*Ryusui Zuki*). Then, drawing the right foot toward the left foot into a natural posture (*Shizentai*), execute a left elbow strike (*Hidari Zempo Enpi Uchi*), while drawing the right fist to the right hip.

Turn to face line 1, and step into a straddle stance (*Sanchin Dachi*), and, drawing the fists to the hips assume a hip posture (*Ryo Goshi Gamae*). Follow this with two parallel fist strikes (*Awaze Zuki*). Draw the right knee up to the chest (*Hasami Uke Hiza Gamae*), and draw the forearms close together and close to the face (*Muso Uke*).

Step with the right foot, line 1, into a front stance (*Zenkutsu Dachi*), and execute a double forearm block (*Kakiwake Uke*). Step with the left foot, line 3, into a front stance (*Zenkutsu Dachi*), and raise the right arm to a high-level blocking position (*Migi Jodan Age Uke*). Drawing the right fist to the right hip, drive the left arm upward to a high-level blocking position (*Hidari Jodan Age Uke*). Then, drawing the left fist to the left hip, drive upward with the right elbow (*Migi Tate Enpi*). Change the stance to a horse riding stance (*Kiba Dachi*), and turn the head to face line 2. Drive the right open hand out and around to the right side of the body until it is fully extended (*Migi Tate Shuto Uke*). Drive the right foot along line 2, making a strike with the heel (*Migi Yoko Geri Kekomi*); return to the horse riding stance (*Kiba Dachi*), and drive the left fist around to the right side of the body to make a middle-level strike (*Hidari Sokumen Zuki*).

Turn the head to face line 3. Drive the left open hand out and around to the left side of the body until it is fully extended (*Hidari Tate Shuto Uke*). Drive the left foot along line 3, making a strike with the heel (*Hidari Yoko Geri Kekomi*); return to the horse riding stance (*Kiba Dachi*), and drive the right fist around to the left side of the body to make a middle-level strike (*Migi Sokumen Zuki*). Turning to face line b, pivot the right wrist clockwise to perform a middle-level block (*Migi Chudan Kake Uke*). Step with the right foot, line b, and drive forward with two palm heel thrusts: the right to low level, and the left to high level (*Teisho Awaze Zuki*).

Turn 180 degrees, and with the left foot forward, line 4, assume a front stance (*Zenkutsu Dachi*). Drive around and upward to a high-level blocking position with the right open hand. Draw the left foot to the right foot into an informal attention stance (*Heisoku Dachi*), and drive the left open hand around to meet the raised right open hand (*Hidari Haishu Age Uchi*); the back of the left hand should be resting against the palm of the right hand. Step backward with the left foot, line b, into a front stance (*Zenkutsu Dachi*). Draw the left hand in an arc past the left side of the body to a point just in front of the groin area. At the same time, drive the right palm heel downward to a point about 6in in front of the left hand (*Koko Hiza Kuzushi*). Change the stance to a fighting stance (*Fudo Dachi*), and drive both fists downward toward the floor (*Gedan Awaze Zuki*).

Turn to face line b and change the stance to a back stance (*Kokutsu Dachi*), then drive the back of the left hand around and outward until it is extended away from the left side of the body (*Hidari Chudan Haishu Uke*). Step with the right foot, line b, into a front stance (*Zenkutsu Dachi*), and drive upward with the right elbow to high level (*Sokumen Tate Enpi*). Make a short sliding movement along line b (*Yori Ashi*), changing the stance to a horse riding stance (*Kiba Dachi*). Draw the right fist to the right shoulder (*Nagashi Uke*), and drive the left fist forward to make a low-level strike (*Hidari Gedan Zuki*). Make a short sliding movement backward along line b and, while drawing the left fist to the left hip, execute a right low-level block (*Migi Sokumen Gedan Barai*).

Turn 180 degrees to face 'start', and change the stance to a back stance (*Kokutsu Dachi*), then drive the back of the left hand around and outward until it is extended away from the left side of the body (*Hidari Chudan Haishu Uke*). Step with the right foot into a horse riding stance (*Kiba Dachi*), and strike the left open palm with the right elbow (*Migi Mae Enpi*). Follow this by facing line a and executing a right low-level block (*Migi Gedan Barai*). Step with the left foot, line a, into a back stance (*Kokutsu Dachi*), and drive the back of the left hand around and outward until it is extended away from the left side of the body (*Hidari Chudan Haishu Uke*).

Step with the right foot, line a, into a front stance (*Zenkutsu Dachi*), and drive upward with the right elbow to high level (*Sokumen Tate Enpi*). Make a short sliding movement along line a (*Yori Ashi*), changing the stance to a horse riding stance (*Kiba Dachi*). Draw the right fist to the right shoulder (*Nagashi Uke*), and drive the left fist forward to make a low-level strike (*Hidari Gedan Zuki*). Make a short sliding movement backward along line a, and, while drawing the left fist to the left hip, execute a right low-level block (*Migi Sokumen Gedan Barai*).

Turning to face 'start', sweep the right foot around in a clockwise semi-circle and step backward with the right foot into a straddle stance (*Sanchin Dachi*), drawing the fists to the hips (*Ryo Goshi Gamae*). Then, drive both fists forward (*Awaze Zuki*): the left fist is at high level and the right fist is at low level. Step with the left foot, line 6f, into a straddle stance (*Sanchin Dachi*), and rotate the arms in a clockwise direction to perform two forearm blocks (*Mawashi Kake Uke*), then, having drawn the fists to the hips, drive forward with the palm heels (*Awaze Teisho Zuki*): the left palm should be at high level and the right palm at low level. Return to *Yoi*.

JIN

From the *Yoi* position, step back with the right foot, line 1, into a front stance (*Zenkutsu Dachi*). At the same time, perform a middle-level block with the left arm (*Hidari Ude Uke*), and a low-level block with the right arm (*Migi Gedan Barai*). Step with the left foot, line 2, into a back stance (*Kokutsu Dachi*). Lower the left arm to a low-level blocking position, and raise the right arm to a high-level blocking position to the right of the body, an 'L' shape (*Manji Gamae*). Pivoting on the heels, turn 180 degrees to face line 3, and assume a back stance (*Kokutsu Dachi*). Lower the right arm to a low-level blocking position, and raise the left arm to a high-level blocking position to the left of the body, an 'L' shape (*Manji Gamae*). Turn to face line 4 and raise the right open hand to a high-level blocking position (*Migi Haishu Age Uke*), followed by the same action with the left arm (*Hidari Age Uke*). Step with the right foot, line 4, into a front stance (*Zenkutsu Dachi*), and execute a right front punch (*Migi Oi Zuki*).

Turn to face line 5 and drive the left open hand to a high-level blocking position (*Hidari Haishu Age Uke*), followed by the same action with the right arm (*Migi Age Uke*). Step with the left foot, line 5, into a front stance (*Zenkutsu Dachi*), and execute a left front punch (*Hidari Oi Zuki*). Step across with the left foot to line 6f into a front stance (*Zenkutsu Dachi*), and execute a left arm low-level block (*Hidari Gedan Barai*).

Step with the right foot, line 6f, and, raising the back of the right hand to the right temple, drive forward with a right knife hand high-level strike (*Migi Jodan Shuto Uke*). Follow this by a step with the left foot, line 6f, and, raising the back of the left hand to the left temple, drive forward with a left knife hand high-level strike (*Hidari Jodan Shuto Uke*). Follow this once again by a step with the right foot, line 6f, and, raising the back of the right hand to the right temple, drive forward with a right knife hand high-level strike (*Migi Jodan Shuto Uke*).

Turn anti-clockwise to face line 10 and step with the left foot into a front stance (*Zenkutsu Dachi*). At the same time, push both forearms forward to perform an opening block (*Kakiwake Uke*). Drive the right foot forward to make a front kick (*Migi Mae Geri*), then step forward with the right foot, line 10, into a front stance (*Zenkutsu Dachi*), and execute a right middle-level punch (*Migi Oi Zuki*), followed by a left middle-level punch (*Hidari Gyaku Zuki*), and continue by making a middle-level blocking action with the right arm (*Migi Ude Uke*) and a low-level blocking action with the left arm (*Hidari Gedan Barai*). Turn clockwise to face line 9 and step with the right foot, line 9, into a front stance (*Zenkutsu Dachi*), at the same time pushing both forearms forward to perform an opening block (*Kakiwake Uke*). Drive the left foot forward to make a front kick (*Hidari Mae Geri*), then step forward with the left foot, line 9, into a front stance (*Zenkutsu Dachi*), and execute a left middle-level punch (*Hidari Oi Zuki*), followed by a right middle-level punch (*Migi Gyaku Zuki*), and continue by making a middle-level blocking action with the right arm (*Migi Ude Uke*) and a low-level blocking action with the left arm (*Hidari Gedan Barai*).

Turning clockwise, sweep the right foot around to line 6r and step into a horse riding stance (*Kiba Dachi*), then execute a right low-level block (*Migi Gedan Barai*). Turn 180 degrees anti-clockwise and sweep the left foot around to line 6r, step into a horse riding stance and execute a left low-

level block (*Hidari Gedan Barai*). Turning clockwise, sweep the right foot around to line 6r and step into a horse riding stance (*Kiba Dachi*), then execute a right low-level block (*Migi Gedan Barai*).

Step diagonally to line b with the left foot into a front stance (*Zenkutsu Dachi*), and drive the left open hand from the right shoulder to the front until it is extended (*Hidari Tate Shuto Uke*). Execute a right middle-level punch (*Hidari Chudan Gyaku Zuki*), followed by a left middle-level punch (*Hidari Chudan Zuki*). Drive forward with the right foot to make a front kick (*Migi Mae Geri*), then step back with the right foot to resume the front stance (*Zenkutsu Dachi*), and make a right middle-level punch (*Migi Chudan Gyaku Zuki*). Make a middle-level blocking action with the right arm (*Migi Ude Uke*), and a low-level blocking action with the left arm (*Hidari Gedan Barai*).

Stepping backward with the left foot, turn anti-clockwise to face line 6f. Lower the right arm to a low-level blocking position, and the left arm to a middle-level blocking position (*Chudan Kosa Uke*). Immediately follow this by dropping the left arm into a low-level blocking action (*Morote Gedan Uke*), then raise both arms upward, allowing them to cross at the solar plexus, and move them out to either side to perform an opening block (*Kakiwake Uke*). Drive the left fist to make a high-level punch (*Hidari Jodan Zuki*), then the right fist to make a middle-level punch (*Migi Chudan Zuki*). Draw the left foot to the right foot and return to *Yoi*.

WANKAN

Look toward line 4, and step with the right over the left foot, then step with the left foot along line 4 into a cat stance (*Neko Ashi Dachi*). At the same time, push both forearms forward to perform an opening block (*Kakiwake Uke*). Sweep across with the left foot to line 5 (*Shaho Sashi Ashi*), then step with the right foot along line 5 into a cat stance (*Neko Ashi Dachi*). At the same time, push both forearms forward to perform an opening block (*Kakiwake Uke*). Turning to face line 6f, draw the right knee up to the chest (*Hasami Uke Hiza Gamae*), and draw the forearms together close to the face (*Muso Uke*). Make three driving steps forward along line 6f, first with the right foot, then the left foot, and once again with the right foot into a front stance (*Zenkutsu Dachi*). At the end of the driving steps, draw the right fist to the right hip, and drive the left open hand forward from the right shoulder until it is extended to the front of the body (*Hidari Tate Shuto Uke*), then drive the right fist forward to execute a middle-level punch (*Migi Chudan Zuki*), followed by a left fist middle-level punch (*Hidari Chudan Zuki*). Turn anti-clockwise to face line 11, and draw the left foot in front of the right foot into a cat stance (*Neko Ashi Dachi*). At the same time, sweep the left open hand around and down to the left to a low-level blocking position, and drive the right open hand forward to a point just in front of the left hand (*Koko Hiza Kuzushi*).

Step with the right foot, line 11, into a front stance (*Zenkutsu Dachi*), and drive the left open hand from the right shoulder to the front until it is extended (*Hidari Tate Shuto Uke*). Follow this by making a right middle-level punch (*Migi Chudan Zuki*), and a left middle-level punch (*Hidari Chudan Gyaku Zuki*). Pivoting on the right foot, turn anti-clockwise to face line 10, and sweep the left foot around and toward

the right foot into a cat stance (*Neko Ashi Dachi*). At the same time, sweep the left open hand around and down to the left to a low-level blocking position, and drive the right open hand forward to a point just in front of the left hand (*Koko Hiza Kuzushi*). Step with the right foot, line 10, into a front stance (*Zenkutsu Dachi*), and drive the left open hand from the right shoulder to the front until it is extended (*Hidari Tate Shuto Uke*). Follow this by making a right middle-level punch (*Migi Chudan Zuki*), and a left middle-level punch (*Hidari Chudan Gyaku Zuki*). Draw the right foot across to line 6r and step into a horse riding stance (*Kiba Dachi*). Draw the left fist to the left hip and drive the right fist from the left hip to the right side of the body to make an upper level hammer fist strike (*Migi Jodan Tettsui Uchi*).

Turn clockwise to face line 6r, and drive forward with the left fist to make a high-level strike (*Hidari Jodan Zuki*). Follow this by driving with the left foot to make a front kick (*Hidari Mae Geri*), then stepping with the left foot along line 6r into a front stance (*Zenkutsu Dachi*). Repeat this action by driving forward with the right fist to make a high-level strike (*Migi Jodan Zuki*), and driving with the right foot to make a front kick (*Migi Mae Geri*), then stepping with the right foot along line 6r into a front stance (*Zenkutsu Dachi*). Follow this once more by driving forward with the left fist to make a high-level strike (*Hidari Jodan Zuki*), and driving with the left foot to make a front kick (*Hidari Mae Geri*), then stepping with the left foot along line 6r into a front stance (*Zenkutsu Dachi*). Pivoting on the feet, turn 180 degrees to face line 6f, and, as the body weight is transferred to the right leg to confirm into a front stance (*Zenkutsu Dachi*), allow the body to bend slightly forward and drive both fists forward, the left at high level and the right at low level (*Yama Zuki*). Draw the right foot back and return to *Yoi*.

CHINTE

From the *Yoi* position, draw the left foot to the right foot into an informal attention stance (*Heisoku Dachi*). Draw the left fist to the solar plexus with the fingers directed upward, and move the right fist to rest on top of the left with the fingers directed toward the body. With the right hand, draw a large semi-circle upward and outward to the right side of the body until the arm is fully extended (*Migi Tettsui Uchi*). Then, draw the right fist under the left fist, and with the left hand draw a large semi-circle out to the left side of the body until the arm is fully extended (*Migi Tettsui Uchi*). Turning to face line 3, step with the left foot, line 6f, into a horse riding stance. At the same time, open the hands, and, allowing the index fingers to touch, drive both hands up to a high-level blocking position (*Awaze Shuto Age Uke*).

Turning to face line 1, change the stance to a fighting stance (*Fudo Dachi*), while drawing the left fist to the left hip and driving the right open hand from the left shoulder out to the front (*Migi Tate Shuto Uke*). Strike the right open palm with the left fist (*Hidari Tate Ken Gyaku Zuki*). Step with the left foot, line 1, into a fighting stance (*Fudo Dachi*), and, while drawing the right fist to the right hip, drive the left open hand from the right shoulder out to the front (*Hidari Tate Shuto Uke*). Strike the left open palm with the right fist (*Hidari Tate Ken Gyaku Zuki*). Step with the right foot, line 1, into a fighting stance (*Fudo Dachi*), and, while drawing the left fist to

the left hip, drive the right open hand from the left shoulder out to the front (*Migi Tate Shuto Uke*). Then, strike the right open hand with the left elbow (*Tate Enpi Zuki*). Turn 180 degrees to face line 6f, and change the stance to a back stance (*Kokutsu Dachi*), then execute a left middle-level knife hand block (*Hidari Shuto Uke*). Step with the right foot, line 6f, into a back stance (*Kokutsu Dachi*), and execute a right middle-level knife hand block (*Migi Shuto Uke*). Drive forward with the left foot to make a middle-level kick (*Hidari Mae Geri*), then step back with the left foot to resume the stance, and execute a right middle-level forearm block (*Migi Ude Uke*). Draw the left foot to the right foot, and, bending at the knees, make a large, low scooping circle with the right arm, from the left to the right side of the body, above the head and down to the right side of the body (*Naiwan Sukui Nage*). As the arm completes the 360-degree circle, drive the right fist down to low level to perform a hammer fist strike (*Migi Gedan Tettsui Uchi*). While stepping back with the right foot, line 6r, into a straddle stance (*Sochin Dachi*), make a large left-to-right circular movement with the open hands (*Morote Kaishu Gedan Uke*). At this point the attention should be directed along line 6f, with the open hands facing the same direction in low-level posture.

Turn to face line 6r and move the body weight over the left leg to assume a back stance (*Kokutsu Dachi*). At the same time, rotate both open hands in a large right to left circle (*Morote Kaishu Gedan Uke*). At this point the attention should be directed along line 6r, with the open hands facing the same direction in low-level posture. Turn to face line 3, and change the stance to a horse riding stance (*Kiba Dachi*). Draw both arms upward across the solar plexus and out to the sides to perform two middle-level blocks (*Ryowan Uchi Uke*). Draw the right foot to a position just behind the left knee (*Tsuru Ashi Dachi*), and extend the arms out to either side in low-level blocking positions (*Ryowan Gamae*). While stepping with the right foot, line 3, rotate the right arm in a large anti-clockwise circle past the right side of the body, and strike downward with the knuckle of the right fist (*Ippon Ken Furi Otoshi*). The right fist should be closed tightly, with the second knuckle protruding. Follow this immediately with the same action using the left arm (*Gyaku Ippon Ken Furi Otoshi*). Then, while drawing the left fist to the left hip, perform a middle-level forearm block with the right arm, with the first two fingers extended in a 'V' shape (*Migi Uchi Uke Nihon Nukite*). Step with the left foot, line 3, and drive forward with the first two fingers of the left hand to a high-level striking position (*Hidari Nihon Nukite*).

Turn 180 degrees anti-clockwise to face line 2, and perform a middle-level forearm block with the first two fingers extended (*Migi Uchi Uke Nihon Nukite*), then step forward with the right foot into a front stance (*Zenkutsu Dachi*), and drive forward with the first two fingers of the right hand to a high-level striking position (*Migi Nihon Nukite*). Turn to face line 1 and step with the right foot into a front stance (*Zenkutsu Dachi*), then drive the right palm heel forward to make a middle-level strike (*Migi Teisho Uchi*), and follow this with the same action using the left palm heel (*Gyaku Teisho Uchi*). After this, strike to the rear with both fists using the second knuckle to make two middle-level strikes (*Ushiro Nakadaka Ippon Ken*). Sliding the left foot across a little, turn 180 degrees to face line

6f, and, using the second knuckle on each fist, drive around and forward to make two middle-level strikes (*Nakadaka Ippon Ken*).

Step with the right foot, line 6f, into a fighting stance (*Fudo Dachi*), and, driving with the right open hand from the left shoulder, make a right knife hand middle-level block (*Migi Tate Shuto Uke*), then strike the right open palm with the left fist (*Hidari Tate Ken Gyaku Zuki*). Step with the left foot, line 6f, into a fighting stance (*Fudo Dachi*), and, driving with the left open hand from the right shoulder, make a left knife hand middle-level block (*Hidari Tate Shuto Uke*), then strike the left open palm with the right fist (*Migi Tate Ken Gyaku Zuki*). After the strike, keep the right fist cupped in the left hand. Draw the left foot to the right foot into an informal attention stance (*Heisoku Dachi*), and make two or three short backward jumps to return to *Yoi*.

UNSU

From an informal attention stance, draw the open hands together to meet at their outer edges by the lower abdomen. Draw the palms upward to a point level with the chest, then drive the palms out to either side of the body (*Kaiun No Te*). Stepping toward line 6f, make a small inward winding circle with the right foot, finishing in a cat stance (*Neko Ashi Dachi*). At the same time, draw the thumb edges of the hands upward to a point level with the solar plexus (*Morote Keito Uke*). With the index fingers extended, drive the right hand forward to make a middle-level strike (*Migi Ippon Nukite*). Stepping toward line 6f, make a small inward winding circle with the left foot, finishing in a cat stance (*Neko Ashi Dachi*), and drive the left hand

53

forward to make a middle-level strike (*Hidari Ippon Nukite*). Stepping toward line 6f, make a small inward winding circle with the right foot, finishing in a cat stance (*Neko Ashi Dachi*), and drive the right hand forward to make a middle-level strike (*Migi Ippon Nukite*).

Step with the left foot, line 7, into a front stance (*Zenkutsu Dachi*). Drive the left open hand from the right shoulder outward until it is level with the left shoulder (*Hidari Tate Shuto Uke*), and follow this with a right middle-level fist strike (*Migi Gyaku Chudan Zuki*). Turn to face line 8, and transfer the weight to the right leg. Drive the right open hand from the left shoulder outward until it is level with the right shoulder (*Migi Tate Shuto Uke*), and follow this with a left middle-level fist strike (*Hidari Gyaku Chudan Zuki*). Step with the left foot, line 6f, into a front stance (*Zenkutsu Dachi*). Drive the left open hand from the right shoulder outward until it is level with the left shoulder (*Hidari Tate Shuto Uke*), and follow this with a right middle-level fist strike (*Migi Gyaku Chudan Zuki*). Turn to face line 6r, and transfer the weight to the right leg. Drive the right open hand from the left shoulder outward until it is level with the right shoulder (*Migi Tate Shuto Uke*), and follow this with a left middle-level fist strike (*Hidari Gyaku Chudan Zuki*).

While directing the attention to line 6r, drop down on to the right hip and place the open hands on the floor to support the body (*Migi Tai Otoshi*), then strike to middle level with the left foot (*Hidari Kasei Geri*). Using the hands and the right foot, flip over to the left hip (*Hidari Tai Otoshi*), and strike to middle level with the right foot (*Migi Kasei Geri*). Rise up from the floor and, facing line 2 but directing the attention to line 6f, step with the right foot,

line 6f, into a horse riding stance (*Kiba Dachi*), and push both palms out to either side of the body (*Kaiun No Te*). Draw the right foot to the left foot, and, pivoting on the right foot, step along line 6f with the left foot into a front stance (*Zenkutsu Dachi*). Using the thumb edge of the hand, drive the left hand in an outward arc to the front at high level (*Hidari Keito Uke*), and at the same time, using the heel of the hand, drive the right hand to the rear in a low-level blocking position (*Migi Ushiro Teisho Barai*). Repeat this action by drawing the left foot to the right foot, and, pivoting on the left foot, step along line 6f with the right foot into a front stance (*Zenkutsu Dachi*). Using the thumb edge of the hand, drive the right hand in an outward arc to the front at high level (*Migi Keito Uke*), and at the same time, using the heel of the hand, drive the left hand to the rear in a low-level blocking position (*Hidari Ushiro Teisho Barai*).

Using the thumb edge of the hand, drive the left hand in an outward arc to the front at high level (*Hidari Keito Uchi*), and at the same time, using the heel of the hand, drive the left hand to the rear in a low-level blocking position (*Hidari Ushiro Teisho Barai*). Driving with the left foot, make a middle-level kick (*Hidari Mae Geri*), and draw the foot back to the right knee. Standing on one leg (*Ippon Dachi*), pivot on the ball of the right foot and make a 180-degree turn to face line 6r. Draw the right fist to the right hip and execute a left middle-level forearm block (*Hidari Chudan Soto Uke*). While stepping backward with the right foot along line 6f, execute a right reverse middle-level punch (*Migi Chudan Gyaku Zuki*).

Sliding the left foot across slightly, turn 180 degrees to face line 6f. Using the thumb edge of the hand, drive the right hand in an outward arc to the front at high-level (*Migi Keito Uke*), and at the same time, using the heel of the hand, drive the left hand to the rear in a low-level blocking position (*Hidari Ushiro Teisho Barai*). Driving with the right foot, make a middle-level kick (*Migi Mae Geri*), and draw the foot back to the right knee. Standing on one leg (*Ippon Dachi*), pivot on the ball of the left foot and make a 180-degree turn to face line 6f. Draw the left fist to the left hip, and execute a right middle-level forearm block (*Migi Chudan Soto Uke*). While stepping backward with the left foot along line 6r, execute a left reverse middle-level punch (*Hidari Chudan Gyaku Zuki*).

Draw the left foot back to the right foot into an informal attention stance (*Heisoku Dachi*), and extend both hands out to either side of the body (*Ryowan Gamae*). Turning to line 8, raise the left hand to high level, then push downward. At the same time, raise the right fist to head height. Step with the right foot, line 8, into a front stance (*Zenkutsu Dachi*), and drive the right fist down to a low-level position. Turn 180 degrees anti-clockwise to face line 7, and, shifting the body weight over the left leg, execute a left low-level block (*Hidari Gedan Barai*). Immediately follow this by turning 180 degrees clockwise to face line 8, transfer the body weight to the right leg and execute a right low-level block (*Migi Gedan Barai*). Turn 180 degrees anti-clockwise to face line 7 and change to a back stance (*Kokutsu Dachi*). Drive the left open hand from the right shoulder out to the front until it is level with the left shoulder (*Hidari Tate Shuto Uke*). While changing to a front stance (*Zenkutsu Dachi*), sweep the right open hand upward to meet the left open hand (*Teisho Tate Hasami Uchi*).

Drive upward and forward with the right knee until it is level with the chest (*Hasami Uke Hiza Gamae*), then drive the heel downward and outward to a low-level striking position (*Gedan Kesage*). Step forward with the right foot, line 7, into a front stance (*Zenkutsu Dachi*), and execute a right middle-level strike (*Migi Chudan Zuki*), followed by a left middle-level punch (*Hidari Chudan Gyaku Zuki*).

Turning anti-clockwise, step across with the right foot, line 6r, into a horse riding stance (*Kiba Dachi*), and execute a right middle-level hammer fist strike along line 6r (*Migi Chudan Tettsui Uchi*), followed by a left back hand upper level block to the left of the body, line 6f (*Hidari Sokumen Jodan Haito Uke*). Turning clockwise, sweep around with the left leg to line 6r into a horse riding stance (*Kiba Dachi*), and execute a left middle-level hammer fist strike (*Hidari Chudan Tettsui Uchi*), followed by a right back hand upper level block to the right of the body, line 6f (*Migi Sokumen Jodan Haito Uke*), then, drawing the right fist to the right hip, drive across the chest with a reverse punch (*Sokumen Gyaku Zuki*). Make a 360-degree turn, leap high into the air, strike the left open hand with the right foot (*Senpu Tobi Geri*), and land in a low stance with the right knee close to the chest and the palm of the hand on the floor supporting the body (*Ryote Fuse*).

Rising, step toward line 1 with the left foot into a straddle stance (*Sanchin Dachi*). Rotate the open hands in large upper and lower clockwise circles (*Mawashi Kake Uke*), then drive forward with the heels of the palms (*Awaze Teisho Zuki*). Repeat this action by stepping toward line 1 with the right foot into a straddle stance (*Sanchin Dachi*). Rotate the open hands in large clockwise circles (*Mawashi Kake Uke*), then drive forward with the heels of the palms (*Awaze Teisho Zuki*). Turning to face line 6f, transfer the body weight to the left leg, and, at the same time, draw the left fist to the left hip and raise the right open hand to a high-level blocking position (*Migi Haishu Age Uke*). Drawing the right fist to the right hip, drive the left fist to a high-level blocking position (*Hidari Haishu Age Uke*), and then execute a right middle-level reverse punch (*Migi Chudan Gyaku Zuki*). Return to *Yoi*.

GOJU SHI HO DAI

Step forward with the right foot, line 6f, into a front stance (*Zenkutsu Dachi*). Drive the right back fist in an anti-clockwise direction around to the right of the body and down to the front to about chest height (*Migi Uraken Uchi*), and bring the left fist to rest under the right elbow. Step with the left foot, line 4, into a back stance (*Kokutsu Dachi*), and, at the same time, raise both arms out to the front to perform a double forearm block (*Kakiwake Uke*). Step with the left foot over the right foot, then step with the right foot, line 5, into a back stance (*Kokutsu Dachi*), and at the same time, raise both arms out to the front to perform a double forearm block (*Kakiwake Uke*). Step with the right foot over the left foot, then step with the left foot, line 4, into a front stance (*Zenkutsu Dachi*). Drive the left open hand around from the right of the body and extend it to a point level with the left shoulder (*Hidari Chudan Tate Shuto Uke*). Follow this with a right middle-level reverse punch (*Migi Chudan Gyaku Zuki*) and a left middle-level punch (*Hidari Chudan Oi Zuki*). With the right foot, execute a front kick (*Migi Mae Geri*), then step with the right foot, line 4, into a front

stance (*Zenkutsu Dachi*), and execute a right front punch (*Migi Oi Zuki*).

Step with the right leg in the direction of line 5, into a front stance (*Zenkutsu Dachi*). Drive the right open hand around from the left of the body and extend it to a point level with the right shoulder (*Migi Chudan Tate Shuto Uke*). Execute a left middle-level reverse punch (*Hidari Chudan Gyaku Zuki*) followed by a right front punch (*Migi Chudan Oi Zuki*). With the left foot, execute a left front kick (*Hidari Mae Geri*), then step with the left foot in the direction of line 5, and execute a left front punch (*Hidari Oi Zuki*). Face line 6f, and step backward with the left leg, line 6r, into a front stance (*Zenkutsu Dachi*), and, while drawing the left fist to the left hip, drive the right elbow upward to high level (*Migi Tate Enpi*).

Turn 180 degrees anti-clockwise, line 6r, into a back stance (*Kokutsu Dachi*). Reach forward with the open hands and draw them back to perform a middle-level blocking action (*Kaishu Kosa Gamae*). Step with the right foot, line 6r, into a front stance (*Zenkutsu Dachi*), and drive the straightened fingers of the right open hand forward to make a middle-level strike (*Migi Nihon Nukite*). Follow this same action with the left fingers (*Hidari Nihon Nukite*), and then again with the right fingers (*Migi Nihon Nukite*). Turn 180 degrees anti-clockwise and step with the left foot, line 6r, into a back stance (*Kokutsu Dachi*). Reach forward with the open hands and draw them back to perform a middle-level blocking action (*Kaishu Kosa Gamae*). Step with the right foot, line 6f, into a front stance (*Zenkutsu Dachi*), and drive the straightened fingers of the right open hand forward to make a middle-level strike (*Migi Nihon Nukite*). Follow this same action with the left fingers

(*Hidari Nihon Nukite*), and then again with the right fingers (*Migi Nihon Nukite*).

Make a three-quarter turn anti-clockwise and step with the left foot, line 8, into a horse riding stance (*Kiba Dachi*), then drive the open hands to the left side of the body (*Morote Kaishu Gedan Uke*). Step with the right foot over the left foot, line 8, into a crossed stance (*Kosa Dachi*). Then drive the left foot forward to make a front kick (*Hidari Mae Geri*), and immediately afterwards step with the left foot, line 8, into a horse riding stance (*Kiba Dachi*), at the same time raising both hands to head height and drawing them to the left hip (*Hidari Koshi Gamae*). While maintaining the stance, turn the head to line 7, and drive both open hands around and down to the right side of the body (*Morote Kaishu Gedan Uke*).

Step with the left foot over the right foot, line 7, into a crossed stance (*Kosa Dachi*). Then drive forward with the right foot to make a front kick (*Migi Mae Geri*), and step with the right foot, line 7, into a horse riding stance (*Kiba Dachi*), at the same time raising both hands to head height and drawing them to the right hip (*Migi Koshi Gamae*). Step backward with the right foot, line 6f, into a back stance (*Kokutsu Dachi*). Reach forward with the open hands and draw them back to perform a middle-level blocking action (*Kaishu Kosa Gamae*). Step with the right foot, line 6r, into a front stance (*Zenkutsu Dachi*), and drive the straightened fingers of the right open hand forward to make a middle-level strike (*Migi Nihon Nukite*). Follow this same action with the left fingers (*Hidari Nihon Nukite*), and then again with the right fingers (*Migi Nihon Nukite*).

Moving the left foot slightly across, turn 180 degrees anti-clockwise to face line 6f,

and assume a front stance (*Zenkutsu Dachi*). At the same time, draw the left fist to the left hip and drive forward with the right open hand to high level (*Migi Jodan Shuto Uke*).

Step forward with the right foot, line 6f, into a front stance (*Zenkutsu Dachi*), and, while drawing the right hand backward, execute a right middle-level block (*Migi Chudan Uchi Uke*). Maintaining the stance, drive the left open hand forward to high level (*Hidari Jodan Shuto Uke*). Follow this by stepping with the left foot, line 6f, into a front stance (*Zenkutsu Dachi*), and, while drawing the left hand backward, execute a left middle-level block (*Hidari Chudan Uchi Uke*). Draw the left fist to the left hip, and drive forward from the left shoulder with the right fist to execute a right middle-level block (*Migi Uchi Uke*). Drive forward with the right foot, line 6f, to make a right front kick (*Migi Mae Geri*), then step with the right foot into a front stance (*Zenkutsu Dachi*). Draw the left foot to the right side of the right foot, line 6f, into a crossed stance (*Kosa Dachi*). At the same time draw the right fist to the left shoulder (*Migi Nagashi Uke*), and drive the left fist under the right elbow to make a middle-level punch (*Hidari Chudan Zuki*).

Step backward with the left foot, line 6r, and, while turning the body to line 6r, look to line 6f, draw the left fist to the left hip and drive the right fist down to a low-level blocking position (*Ushiro Gedan Barai*).

Turn the head to face line 6r, and, transferring the body weight to the right leg, assume a back stance (*Kokutsu Dachi*). Reach forward with the open hands and draw them back to perform a middle-level blocking action (*Kaishu Kosa Gamae*).

Step with the right foot, line 6f, into a front stance (*Zenkutsu Dachi*), and drive the straightened fingers of the right open hand forward to make a middle-level strike (*Migi Nihon Nukite*). Follow this same action with the left fingers (*Hidari Nihon Nukite*), and then again with the right fingers (*Migi Nihon Nukite*). Make a three-quarter turn anti-clockwise and step with the left foot, line 7, into a horse riding stance (*Kiba Dachi*). At the same time, drive both open hands around and down to the left side of the body (*Morote Kaishu Gedan Uke*).

Step with the right foot over the left foot, line 7, into a crossed stance (*Kosa Dachi*), then drive forward with the left foot to make a middle-level kick (*Hidari Mae Geri*), and step along line 7 into a horse riding stance (*Kiba Dachi*). Immediately after the kick, drive around and forward with the left open hand (*Hidari Jodan Tate Shuto Uke*), then, pulling the left hand back to the left hip, drive forward with the right fist to make a middle-level punch (*Migi Chudan Zuki*). Follow this by driving both open hands around and down to the right side of the body (*Morote Kaishu Gedan Uke*).

Step with the left foot over the right, line 8, into a crossed stance (*Kosa Dachi*). Drive forward with the right foot to make a middle-level front kick (*Migi Mae Geri*), then step with the right foot, line 8, into a horse riding stance (*Kiba Dachi*). Immediately after the kick, drive around and forward with the left open hand (*Hidari Jodan Tate Shuto Uke*), then, pulling the left hand back to the left hip, drive forward with the right fist to make a middle-level punch (*Migi Chudan Zuki*). Step with the right foot, line 6f, into a front stance (*Zenkutsu Dachi*), then, rotating the right fist anti-clockwise upward past the right shoulder and downward to middle level, make a back fist strike (*Migi Uraken Uchi*). Step backward with the right foot, line 6r, into a horse riding stance (*Kiba Dachi*). Draw the left fist to the left hip and drive it around to the left side of the body to make a hammer fist strike (*Hidari Chudan Tettsui Uchi*). Step with the right foot, line 6f, into a front stance (*Zenkutsu Dachi*), and execute a right middle-level punch (*Migi Chudan Oi Zuki*).

Look to line 7. Draw the right foot to the left foot into an informal attention stance (*Heisoku Dachi*), and drive both fists out away from the body (*Ryo Wan Zenpo Nobashi*), then, bending the body slightly forward, drive the fists out and around to the rear of the body to make two hammer fists strikes (*Ushiro Tettsui Hasami Uchi*). Pivoting on the balls of the feet, turn to line 6r and position the fists firmly on the hips with the elbows directed out to either side of the body (*Ryoken Koshi Gamae*). Draw a small clockwise semi-circle with the right foot while stepping forward, line 6r, into a cat stance (*Neko Ashi Dachi*), and extend both open hands to either side of the body at a low-level position (*Ryo Kaishu Gamae*). Following smoothly from this, draw both thumb edges of the hands upward and forward to about middle level (*Morote Keito Uke*). Step forward with the right foot and draw the left foot up behind it into a cat stance (*Neko Ashi Dachi*). Draw both hands together so the palm heels are touching with the fingers pointing out to either side, and drive them forward, line 6r, to perform an ox jaw block (*Morote Seiryuto Uchi*). Turn 180 degrees anti-clockwise and step back with the right foot into a back stance (*Kokutsu Dachi*). Reach forward with the open hands and draw them back to perform a middle-level blocking action (*Kaishu Kosa Gamae*). Draw the left foot to the right foot and return to *Yoi*.

GOJU SHI HO SHO

Step forward with the right foot, line 6f, into a front stance (*Zenkutsu Dachi*). Drive the right fist in an anti-clockwise direction around to the right of the body and down to the front to about chest height (*Migi Uraken Uchi*), then bring the left fist to rest under the right elbow. Step with the left foot, line 4, into a front stance (*Zenkutsu Dachi*), and, at the same time, drive both fists out to the front to perform a double fist strike (*Heiko Tate Zuki*). Step with the right foot, line 5, into a front stance (*Zenkutsu Dachi*), and, at the same time, drive both fists out to the front to perform a double fist strike (*Heiko Tate Zuki*). Step with the right foot over the left foot, then step with the left foot, line 4, into a front stance (*Zenkutsu Dachi*). Drive the left open hand around from the right of the body and extend it to a point level with the left shoulder (*Hidari Chudan Tate Shuto Uke*). Follow this with a right middle-level reverse punch (*Migi Chudan Gyaku Zuki*), and a left middle-level punch (*Hidari Chudan Oi Zuki*).

With the right foot, execute a front kick (*Migi Mae Geri*), then step back with the right foot, line 4, into a front stance (*Zenkutsu Dachi*), and execute a right front punch (*Migi Chudan Gyaku Zuki*). Step with the right leg in the direction of line 5 into a front stance (*Zenkutsu Dachi*). Drive the right open hand around from the left of the body and extend it to a point level with the right shoulder (*Migi Chudan Tate Shuto Uke*). Execute a left middle-level reverse punch (*Hidari Chudan Gyaku Zuki*) followed by a right front punch (*Migi Chudan Oi Zuki*). With the left foot, execute a left front kick (*Hidari Mae Geri*), then step back with the left foot in the direction of line 5, and execute a left front punch (*Hidari Chudan Gyaku Zuki*).

Face line 6f and step across with the right leg, line 6f, into a front stance (*Zenkutsu Dachi*), then, while drawing the left fist to the left hip, drive the right elbow upward to high level (*Migi Tate Enpi*). Turn 180 degrees anti-clockwise and sweep around with the right foot, line 6r, into a cat stance (*Neko Ashi Dachi*), raise the thumb edge of the right hand to a middle-level blocking position with the index finger extended, and the back of the left open hand resting under the right elbow. Lower the left open hand to a low-level blocking position, and raise the right hand to a high level ready to make a one-finger strike. Step with the right foot, line 6r, into a front stance (*Zenkutsu Dachi*), and drive the straightened finger of the right hand forward to make a middle-level strike (*Migi Ippon Nukite*). Follow this same action with the left finger (*Hidari Ippon Nukite*), and then again with the right finger (*Migi Ippon Nukite*).

Turn 180 degrees anti-clockwise and step with the right foot, line 6f, into a cat stance (*Neko Ashi Dachi*), raise the thumb edge of the right hand to a middle-level blocking position with the index finger extended and the back of the left open hand resting under the right elbow. Lower the left open hand to a low-level blocking position, and raise the right hand to a high level ready to make a one-finger strike. Step with the right foot, line 6r, into a front stance (*Zenkutsu Dachi*), and drive the straightened finger of the right hand forward to make a middle-level strike (*Migi Ippon Nukite*). Follow this same action with the left finger (*Hidari Ippon Nukite*), and then again with the right finger (*Migi Ippon Nukite*). Make a three-quarter turn anti-clockwise and step with the left foot, line 8, into a horse riding stance (*Kiba Dachi*), and drive the open hands to the left side of the body (*Morote Kaishu Gedan Uke*). Step with the right foot over the left foot, line 8, into a crossed stance (*Kosa Dachi*). Then drive the left foot forward to make a front kick (*Hidari Mae Geri*), and immediately afterwards step with the left foot, line 8, into a horse riding stance (*Kiba Dachi*), at the same time raising both hands to head height and drawing them to the left hip (*Hidari Koshi Gamae*).

While maintaining the stance, turn the head to line 7, and drive both open hands around and down to the right side of the body (*Morote Kaishu Gedan Uke*). Step with the left foot over the right foot, line 7, into a crossed stance (*Kosa Dachi*). Then, drive forward with the right foot to make a front kick (*Migi Mae Geri*), and step with the right foot, line 7, into a horse riding stance (*Kiba Dachi*), at the same time raising both hands to head height and drawing them to the left hip (*Migi Koshi Gamae*).

Sweep across with the right foot to line 6r into a cat stance (*Neko Ashi Dachi*), raise the thumb edge of the right hand to a middle-level blocking position with the index finger extended and the back of the left open hand resting under the right elbow. Lower the left open hand to a low-level blocking position, and raise the right hand to a high level, ready to make a one-finger strike. Step with the right foot, line 6r, into a front stance (*Zenkutsu Dachi*), and drive the straightened finger of the right hand forward to make a middle-level strike (*Migi Ippon Nukite*). Follow this same action with the left finger (*Hidari Ippon Nukite*), and then again with the right finger (*Migi Ippon Nukite*).

Moving the left foot slightly across, turn 180 degrees anti-clockwise to face line 6f,

and assume a front stance (*Zenkutsu Dachi*). At the same time, draw the left fist to the left hip and drive forward with the right open hand to low level (*Migi Gedan Teishu Uke*). Step forward with the right foot, line 6f, into a front stance (*Zenkutsu Dachi*). Draw the right hand backward in a small circular action, then drive forward with the right back fist and execute a right middle-level hammer fist strike (*Migi Chudan Uraken Uchi*). Maintaining the stance, drive the left open hand forward to low level (*Hidari Gedan Teishu Uke*). Follow this by stepping with the left foot, line 6f, into a front stance (*Zenkutsu Dachi*), and, while drawing the left hand backward, drive forward with the left back fist and execute a left middle-level hammer fist strike (*Hidari Chudan Uraken Uchi*).

Step forward with the right foot, line 6f, into a front stance (*Zenkutsu Dachi*). Pressing the right thumb and fingertips tightly together, use them to strike downward to middle level (*Washite Otoshi Uchi*). Follow this by lowering the right hand and reversing the direction of the strike upwards (*Washite Age Uchi*).

Drive forward with the left foot, line 6f, to make a right front kick (*Migi Mae Geri*). At the same time, draw the right fist to the left shoulder (*Migi Nagashi Uke*), and drive the left fist under the right elbow to make a middle-level punch (*Hidari Chudan Zuki*), then draw the left foot back, line 6r, and, while turning the body to line 6r, look to line 6f, drive the left elbow to a high-level position along line 6r, and drive the right fist down to a low-level blocking position, line 6f (*Ushiro Gedan Barai*).

Turn the head to face line 6r, and sweep the right leg toward line 6r to assume a cat stance (*Neko Ashi Dachi*). Raise the thumb edge of the right hand to a middle-level blocking position with the index finger extended and the back of the left open hand resting under the right elbow. Lower the left open hand to a low-level blocking position, and raise the right hand to a high level, ready to make a one-finger strike. Push forward with the right foot, line 6r, into a front stance (*Zenkutsu Dachi*), and drive the straightened finger of the right hand forward to make a middle-level strike (*Migi Ippon Nukite*). Follow this same action with the left finger (*Hidari Ippon Nukite*), and then again with the right finger (*Migi Ippon Nukite*).

Make a three-quarter turn anti-clockwise and step with the left foot, line 7, into a horse riding stance (*Kiba Dachi*). At the same time, drive both open hands around and down to the left side of the body (*Morote Kaishu Gedan Uke*). Step with the right foot over the left foot, line 7, into a crossed stance (*Kosa Dachi*), then drive forward with the left foot to make a middle-level kick (*Hidari Mae Geri*), and step along line 7 into a horse riding stance (*Kiba Dachi*). Immediately after the kick, drive around and forward with the left open hand (*Hidari Jodan Tate Shuto Uke*), then, pulling the left hand back to the left hip, drive forward with the right fist to make a middle-level punch (*Migi Chudan Zuki*). Follow this by driving both open hands around and down to the right side of the body (*Morote Kaishu Gedan Uke*).

Step with the left foot over the right, line 8, into a crossed stance (*Kosa Dachi*). Drive forward with the right foot to make a middle-level front kick (*Migi Mae Geri*), then step with the right foot, line 8, into a horse riding stance (*Kiba Dachi*). Immediately after the kick, drive around and forward with the left open hand (*Hidari Jodan Tate Shuto Uke*), then, pulling the left hand back to the left hip, drive forward with the right fist to make a middle-level punch (*Migi Chudan Zuki*). Step with the right foot, line 6f, into a front stance (*Zenkutsu Dachi*), then, rotating the right fist anti-clockwise upward past the right shoulder and downward to middle level, make a back fist strike (*Migi Uraken Uchi*).

Step backward with the right foot, line 6r, into a horse riding stance (*Kiba Dachi*). Draw the left fist to the left hip and drive it around to the left side of the body to make a hammer fist strike (*Hidari Chudan Tettsui Uchi*). Step with the right foot, line 6f, into a front stance (*Zenkutsu Dachi*), and execute a right middle-level punch (*Migi Chudan Oi Zuki*). Look to line 7. Draw the left foot toward the right foot into an informal attention stance (*Heisoku Dachi*), drive both fists forward with the arms parallel (*Ryo Wan Zempo Nobashi*), then, bending the body slightly forward, drive the fists out and around to the rear of the body to make two hammer fists strikes (*Ushiro Tettsui Hasami Uchi*). Draw both fists up close to the nipples (*Suihei Hiji Gamae*), and, while turning to line 6r and stepping into a front stance (*Zenkutsu Dachi*), drive the elbow around while maintaining *Suihei Hiji Gamae*.

Draw a small clockwise semi-circle with the right foot while stepping forward, line 6r, into a cat stance (*Neko Ashi Dachi*), and extend both open hands to either side of the body at a low-level position (*Ryo Kaishu Gamae*). Raise the thumb edge of each hand to a middle-level blocking position with the index fingers extended and pointing downward. Make a short sliding motion (*Yori Ashi*), and drive both fingers downward in a low-level striking action (*Morote Gedan Ippon Nukite*).

Following smoothly from this, turn 180 degrees anti-clockwise, and assume a cat stance with the left foot forward (*Neko Ashi Dachi*). Raise the thumb edge of the right hand to a middle-level blocking position with the index finger extended and the back of the left open hand resting under the right elbow (*Migi Keito Uke*). Draw the left foot to the right foot and return to *Yoi*.

MEIKYO SHO

Look along line 6f and, arching the body slightly forward, drive both fists out to make two middle-level punches (*Ryo Wan Zempo Nobashi*). As the arms are drawn back and the body straightens, step with the right foot, line 3, into a horse riding stance (*Kiba Dachi*), and draw the fists to the hips (*Ryo Goshi Gamae*). Open the hands and raise them to about head height with the palms directed away from the body, then slowly lower them to about chest height (*Joshin Gamae*), and make two large outward winding circles with the arms until they are extended on either side of the body (*Ryowan Gamae*).

Looking to the left, slide 4–6in along line 2 (*Yori Ashi*), and at the same time, make large circular clockwise rotations with both arms and drive the outer edge of each hand out to the left side of the body in low-level positions (*Morote Enshin Haito Barai*). Look to the right and repeat the same actions on the right side, that is slide 4–6in along line 3 (*Yori Ashi*), and at the same time, make large circular anti-clockwise rotations with both arms and drive the outer edge of each hand out to the right side of the body in low-level positions (*Morote Enshin Haito Barai*). Once again slide 4–6in along line 3 (*Yori Ashi*), and drive the outer edge of each hand from the left of the body to the front at low level, then, flipping the hands over, drive the outer edge of each hand out to the left side of the body (*Morote Enshin Haito Barai*).

Look along line 6f and extend the left open hand outward to the front (*Hidari Tate Shuto Uke*), then strike the left open hand with the right elbow (*Migi Mae Enpi Zuki*). Follow this by extending the right arm out to the front (*Migi Tate Shuto Uke*), then, drawing the right fist back to the right hip, thrust forward with a left middle-level punch (*Hidari Chudan Zuki*), immediately retracting the left fist and driving forward with a right middle-level punch (*Migi Chudan Zuki*).

Step forward with the right foot, line 6f, into a back stance (*Kokutsu Dachi*), and execute a right middle-level knife hand block (*Migi Chudan Shuto Uke*). Step forward with the left foot, line 6f, into a front stance (*Zenkutsu Dachi*), and strike the right open hand with the left elbow (*Hidari Mae Enpi Zuki*), followed quickly by driving the left open hand out to the front (*Hidari Tate Shuto Uke*), then stepping forward with the right foot, line 6f, into a front stance (*Zenkutsu Dachi*), and executing a right middle-level punch (*Migi Chudan Zuki*).

Look to line 12, and draw the right foot up to the left knee (*Sagi Ashi Dachi*). Draw the back of the left hand to the left temple and execute a right low-level knife hand block (*Shuto Gedan Barai*), then step with the right foot along line 12 into a back stance (*Kokutsu Dachi*), and, using the thumb edge of the right hand, execute a right middle-level open hand block (*Migi Haito Uchi Uke*). Slide the right foot forward and change to a front stance (*Zenkutsu Dachi*). Drive forward and upward with the right elbow (*Tate Enpi Zuke*), then drive forward with the right fist to make a right high-level punch (*Migi Jodan Zuki*).

Step across with the right foot to line 6f, into a horse riding stance (*Kiba Dachi*), and at the same time execute a right middle-level forearm block (*Migi Uchi Komi*). Slide the right foot along line 6f slightly (*Yori Ashi*), and execute a right low-level block (*Migi Gedan Barai*).

Look to line 11 and draw the right foot up to the left knee (*Sagi Ashi Dachi*), then, using the back of the left hand to cover the temple, execute a right low-level knife hand block (*Shuto Gedan Barai*). Step with the right foot, line 11, into a back stance (*Kokutsu Dachi*), and, using the thumb edge of the right hand, execute a right middle-level open hand block (*Migi Haito Uchi Uke*). Slide the right foot forward and change to a front stance (*Zenkutsu Dachi*). Drive forward and upward with the right elbow (*Tate Enpi Zuke*), then drive forward with the right fist to make a right high-level punch (*Migi Jodan Zuki*). Step along line 11 with the left foot into a horse riding stance (*Kiba Dachi*), and, at the same time, drive the back of the left open hand out to the left side of the body to make a middle-level back hand block (*Haisho Uke*).

Make a large sliding movement toward line 6 (*Yori Ashi*) and step into a horse riding stance (*Kiba Dachi*). Drive both open hands forward and downward to a low level (*Koko Hiza Kuzushi*). Draw the left foot toward the right foot and step into battle stance (*Sanchin Dachi*). Rotate the arms in small clockwise circles and draw the open hands back to the hips (*Mawashi Kake Zuki*). Step forward with the right foot into a front stance (*Zenkutsu Dachi*), and drive both palm heels forward – the left at high level and the right at low level (*Awaze Teisho Zuki*). Change the stance to a horse riding stance, facing line 11, (*Kiba Dachi*), and execute a right low-level block along line 6f (*Migi Gedan Barai*). Turn anti-clockwise to face line 6r and draw the right foot toward the left foot and step into battle stance (*Sanchin Dachi*), and draw the fists to the hips (*Koshi Gamae*). Drive forward with the fists – the left at high level and the right at low level (*Awaze Zuki*). Draw the fists back to the hips, then drive forward with the fists again – the right at high level and the left at low level (*Awaze Zuki*).

Turn 180 degrees anti-clockwise and step backward with the left foot, line 6r, into a back stance (*Kokutsu Dachi*), then execute a right middle-level knife hand block (*Migi Shuto Uke*). Step back with the right foot, line 6r, into a back stance (*Kokutsu Dachi*), and execute a left middle-level knife hand block (*Hidari Shuto Uke*).

While turning 360 degrees, strike the left open hand with the right foot (*Migi Mikazuki Geri*), then step backward with the left foot into a back stance (*Kokutsu Dachi*), and execute a right middle-level knife hand block (*Hidari Shuto Uke*). Step backward with the right foot, line 6r, into a back stance (*Kokutsu Dachi*), and execute a left middle-level knife hand block (*Hidari Shuto Uke*). Draw the left foot to the right foot and return to *Yoi*.

8 Techniques Required for Kata

Fig 14 Age Uke.

AGE UKE

Rising block. Draw the right arm across the stomach so the fist is in alignment with the left side of the chest, fingers facing upward.

Continue by driving the fist upward in alignment with the left side of the chest and face until the arm is 6in above the head. At this point, allow the fist to turn anti-clockwise until the palm is directed away from the body and drive the fist forward 6in. Bending at the wrist, allow the fist to turn upward so the knuckle of the index finger is pointing directly upward.

Fig 15 Age Zuki.

AGE ZUKI

Rising strike. This is a high-level strike. Drive forward with the right fist with the fingers facing upward and the elbow tucked into the body. As the striking fist goes forward the inside of the upper right arm should skim past the right side of the chest. At the end of the strike allow the fist to turn anti-clockwise in a semi-circle until the fingers are directed downward.

ASHI BARAI

Foot sweep. This is a sweeping movement made by the foot. From any stance this involves driving the foot forward and to the side to catch the ankle or leg of the oncoming attacker. Timing is very important as contact needs to be made before the attacker confirms in stance.

AWAZE SHUTO AGE UKE

Join, sword hand rising block. This is a rising block using both open hands. Drive upward with both open hands to a high-level blocking position. Allow the thumbs to touch, and the fingers of the right hand to rest across the back of the fingers of the left hand. The palms should be directed away from the face and angled upward.

Fig 16 Ashi Barai.

Fig 17 Awaze Shuto Age Uke.

AWAZE TEISHO ZUKI

Join, palm heel strike. From any stance drive both palm heels forward, one at high level and the other at low level. The intention here is to strike at the chin or face with one hand, and to the lower abdomen with the other hand.

Fig 19 Awaze Zuki.

Fig 18 Awaze Teisho Zuki.

AWAZE ZUKI

Join, strike. This strike is similar to *Awaze Teisho Zuki* but using fists rather than palm heels.

BO DORI TSUKI OTOSHI

Stick, catch, thrust, dropping. The intention in this instance is to catch a Bo Staff. For example, in a right back stance the left open hand is raised just above the forehead with the back of the hand toward the head, and the right open hand is slightly outstretched at middle level with the palm heel directed forward. Having caught the Bo Staff, the left hand is then drawn downward and the right hand raised very slightly. During this action the hands are twisted over and closed to form fists. At the finish, the fingers of the right fist should be directed downward, and the fingers of the left fist directed upward.

Fig 20 Bo Dori Tsuki Otoshi.

Fig 21 Bo Uke.

BO UKE

Bo catch. This is very similar to the first half of *Bo Dori Tsuki Otoshi* in that the intention is to catch a Bo Staff. For example, in a right back stance the left open hand is raised to just above the forehead with the back of the hand toward the head, and the right open hand is slightly outstretched at middle level with the palm heel directed forward.

DOJI HAITO UCHI

At the same time, back sword hit or strike. From a horse riding stance, draw both hands to the left hip with the left hand

Fig 22 Doji Haito Uchi.

closed and the back of the right open hand resting on top of the left fist. Drive around to the right of the body at middle level with the left hand. The intention here is to strike the attacker using the thumb edge of the left hand. It is important, therefore, to tuck the thumb into the palm of the hand.

ENPI

Enpi simply means elbow. Depending on the intent of the application, all techniques in karate are potentially lethal. This is particularly so with the application of an elbow strike. Even in the absence of intent, accidental contact with a vulnerable part of the attacker's body, such as the face or ribs, can be extremely damaging. The application of this technique in sparring, therefore, should be made using the fleshy part of the arm to the outside of the elbow. This limits the use of Enpi to safe limits.

In reality, that is when required against an aggressive attacker whose intent is to cause actual bodily harm, the bony part of the elbow is applied. In this way, Enpi can be delivered by driving the elbow around from the side of the body to the front, to attack upward and forward from the side of the body to the chin of the attacker, This is an extremely powerful and dangerous application of Enpi as it can break the jaw, break the neck by the sudden jolt backwards, or even kill by driving the attacker's head backwards and breaking the neck.

Additionally, Enpi can be applied by driving the elbow backwards to the attacker's abdomen, solar plexus or lower ribs. Again, this is a very powerful technique requiring caution. A powerful elbow strike to the abdomen can cause severe breathing problems and even cardiac arrest. Likewise, driving the elbow down to the top of an

attacker's head can result in a fractured skull or even brain damage. Not only are such effects undesirable, they are illegal and the excessive use of them, as with any technique, subtracts from the true values and principles of true karate-do.

ENPI UCHI

Elbow strike. Make sure the arm does not obscure the vision.

Fig 23 Enpi Uchi.

FUDO DACHI

Steadfast stance. The position for this stance is similar to front stance, but the back leg is bent and the body is centrally positioned with the weight evenly distributed over both legs.

Fig 24 Fudo Dachi.

GEDEN BARAI

Low-level sweeping block. While in a right front stance, raise the right fist to the left shoulder with the fingers to the side of the face. Drive the back of the fist down to a point about 6in above the right knee. When this point is reached, allow the fist to turn clockwise so the fingers are facing the knee.

Fig 25 Geden Barai.

GEDEN GAMAE

Low-level posture. This posture is very similar to *Gedan Barai* but with a shorter stance.

GYAKU TEISHO UCHI

Reverse palm heel strike. From a right front stance, drive the left palm heel forward to middle level. The fingers of the left hand are directed out to the side of the body.

GYAKU UCHI UKE

Reverse striking block. With the left foot forward in *Sanchin Dachi*, allow the body

Fig 26 Geden Gamae.

Fig 27 Gyaku Teisho Uchi.

Fig 28 Gyaku Uchi Uke.

to twist at the waist and draw the right arm around to make a middle-level forearm block.

GYAKU ZUKI

Reverse strike. Stepping forward into a left front stance, drive the right fist forward to make a middle-level punch. The fist should drive forward with the fingers facing upward and the elbow tucked into the body. As the striking fist goes forward the inside of the upper right arm should skim past the right side of the chest. At the end of the strike allow the fist to turn anti-clockwise until the fingers are directed downward.

Fig 29 Gyaku Zuki.

HAISHO UCHI

Back hand rising block. This is basically a strike with the back of the open hand.

HAISHU AGE UKE

Back hand rising block. Draw both open hands together so the thumbs and index fingers are touching. There should be a triangular space between the thumbs and fingers. Raise both hands to a high-level blocking position.

Fig 30 Haisho Uchi.

Fig 31 Haisho Age Uke.

Fig 32 Haishu Awaze Uke

Fig 33 Haito Sukui Nage (1).

HAISHU AWAZE UKE

Back hand combined block. Raise the hands to head height, and position them back to back. The fingers of the right hand are directed upward and the fingers of the left hand are directed forward.

HAITO SUKUI NAGE

Back sword scooping throw. With the feet together, bend at the knees and move the right open hand out to the left of the body. Scoop downward in front of the body with the right back hand, out to the right side. The intention here is to scoop away a kick or low-level strike.

Fig 34 Haito Sukui Nage (2).

72

Fig 35 Haito Sukui Nage (3).

Fig 36 Hasami Uke.

HANGETSU DACHI

Hour glass stance. This is referred to as the hour glass stance because it concaves at the knees and resembles the profile of an hour glass. Take a step forward with the right foot. Turn the right foot by pivoting on the ball of the foot until the outer edge of the foot is horizontal to the starting point. Test this stance by drawing an imaginary line from the left heel to the right heel, then, following the line of the toes draw another two lines until they meet. This should produce a triangle of space. Bend the knees inward toward each other until the thighs are almost vertically aligned.

HASAMI UKE

Both sides hit or strike. Draw both arms together in front of the face. The fingers are directed toward the face, and the little finger edges are touching. Although the arms are drawn together, there is a slight gap between the wrists which is used to see ahead.

HEIKO TATE ZUKI

Even length, strike. Draw both fists to the hip and drive forward to the middle level with both fists to make a double strike. The fingers of both fists are directed toward each other with the thumbs directed upward.

HEISOKU DACHI

Attention stance. This is a simple stance. The feet are drawn together so the inside edges of each foot are touching. The body is upright, relaxed and ready for action.

Fig 38 Hiji Barai.

Fig 37 Heisoku Dachi.

HIJI BARAI

Arm sweep. While standing in horse riding stance, place both fists on the hips then sweep around to the front with the elbow.

HINERI KAESHI

Twist, return. Step into a right front stance and execute a right middle-level fist strike. Immediately afterwards, perform a middle-level forearm block by slightly withdrawing the right fist toward the left shoulder then twisting the arm around to make the block.

HIRATE OSAE UKE

Open hand palm pressing block. Assume a left front stance. Extend the left arm to make a sword hand block (*Shuto Uke*). Pivoting at the elbow, press downward with the left palm to about middle level. At this

point the forearm is parallel to the body (the fingers are directed to the right side of the body).

HIZA GAMAE

Knee posture. Standing on the left leg, raise the right knee to middle level. Draw both fists upward to a point just in front of the face but do not obscure the vision. The little finger edges of the hands should be touching, and the forearms close together. The fingers of the fists are directed toward the face.

Fig 39 Hineri Kaeshi.

Fig 40 Hirate Osae Uke.

Fig 41 Hiza Gamae.

75

Fig 42 *Ippon Dachi.*

Fig 43 *Ippon Ken Furi Otoshi.*

IPPON DACHI

One stance. In this instance *Ippon Dachi* refers to standing on one leg as a stance.

IPPON KEN FURI OTOSHI

One fist swing, dropping. From a right front stance, swing the right fist in a large anti-clockwise circle at the side of the body. The right fist is first driven downward to the rear of the body, continuing above head height, and finally outstretched to the front at middle level. The knuckles of the right fist should be directed downward.

IPPON KEN GYAKU FURI OTOSHI

Reverse one fist swing, dropping. This can be a follow-on from *Ippon Ken Furi Otoshi.*

Fig 44 *Ippon Ken Gyaku Furi Otoshi.*

From a right front stance, swing the left fist in a large clockwise circle at the side of the body. The left fist is first driven downward to the rear of the body, continuing above head height, and finally outstretched to the front at middle level. The knuckles of the left fist should be directed downward.

IPPON NUKITE

One pierce hand. In this instance, *Ippon Nukite* refers to piercing using one finger. The first finger is extended and the other fingers are bent at the second knuckle so the tips are just touching the top of the palm. The thumb is folded over toward the palm.

JO KUZAMI

Staff, grasp hold of. This can be a follow-on from *Morote Jo Uke*, in that the intention is to catch a Jo Staff. For example, in a right back stance the left open hand is raised to just above the forehead with the back of the hand toward the head, and the right open hand is slightly outstretched at middle level with the palm heel directed forward. Having caught the Jo Staff, the left hand is then drawn downward and the right hand raised very slightly. During this action the hands are twisted over and closed to form fists. At the finish, the fingers of the right fist should be directed downward, and the fingers of the left fist directed upward.

Fig 45 Ippon Nukite.

Fig 46 Jo Kuzami.

JOSHIN GAMAE

Jo, mind or spirit, posture. Assuming a horse riding stance, draw both open hands upward with the palms directed upward and the little finger edges touching. As the palms reach a position level with the face, allow the palms to turn outward away from the face and lower them to about shoulder height.

KAISHU HAIWAN UKE

Open hand back arm block. While standing in back stance, raise the right arm to a high-level position. The right arm should form an 'L' shape, the hand is open, and the thumb edge is directed toward the head.

Fig 48 Kaishu Haiwan Uke.

KAISHU KOSA GAMAE

Open hand crossed posture. Standing in a right back stance, draw the right arm out to

Fig 47 Joshin Gamae.

Fig 49 Kaishu Kosa Gamae.

the left of the body in a 'V' shape with the palm of the open hand directed downward. At the same time, draw the left open hand under the right elbow with the back of the left hand touching the elbow. At this point, allow the right hand to flip over so the palm is facing upward, and perform an open-handed low-level block with the left hand.

KAIUN NO TE

Open cloud hand. From an informal attention stance, draw the open hands together, meeting at the little finger edges by the lower abdomen. Draw the palms upward to a point level with the chest, then drive the palms outward to either side of the body with the fingers directed upward and the palms away from the body.

Fig 50 Kaiun No Te.

KAKE UKE

Suspend block. Standing in a left front stance, draw the right open hand upward toward the chest with the palm directed toward the chest. Using the back of the hand, push away from the chest and downward to about middle level.

Fig 51 Kake Uke.

KAKIWAKE UKE

Wedging block. Move the fists across the body until they cross at the solar plexus. The inside of the right forearm should be just in front of the outside of the left forearm and the fingers of the fists should be facing the body. Continue moving the arms upward and forward and allow them to separate at about shoulder height. Keep the

Fig 52 Kakiwake Uke.

Fig 53 Kasei Geri.

elbows bent and close to the chest. Bring the right fist in line with the right shoulder and the left fist in line with the left shoulder. At this point, allow the fists to turn, the right in an anti-clockwise direction and the left in a clockwise direction, until the fingers are directed forward away from the body.

KASEI GERI

Low force kick. This is a kick made from ground level. Lying on one's left side, place the palms of the hands on to the floor, and draw the left leg upward slightly until it is in a 'V' shape. Draw the right knee up toward the chest and kick high using the ball of the foot.

KASUI KEN

Fire, water, fist. Basically, this is two blocks carried out at the same time – *Ude Uke* and *Gedan Barai*. Assume a left back stance. Drive the left fist down to a low-level blocking position, and draw the right arm in a 'V' shape out to the right of the body.

KEITO UKE

Chicken head block. The first finger is extended and the other fingers are bent at the second knuckle so the tips are just touching the top of the palm. The thumb is folded over toward the palm. The hand is driven upward using the thumb edge to make the block.

KESAGE

Kick down. Raise the right knee upward toward the chest. Allowing the body to twist slightly to the side, drive downward with the outer edge of the foot to a low-level striking position.

Fig 54 Kasui Ken.

Fig 56 Kesage.

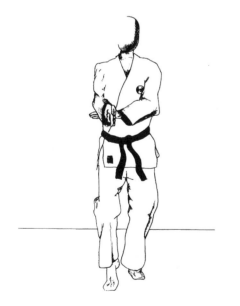

Fig 55 Keito Uke.

KIBA DACHI

Horse riding stance. This stance is referred to as the horse riding stance because of its similarity to the position of the legs when riding a horse. To achieve the correct position, stand with the feet together, then turn the feet outward so the toes are facing 35 degrees to the sides, push the heels out to the side until they are facing 35 degrees away from the body to the rear, and once again turn the feet so the toes are pointing 35 degrees away from the body. Finally, slowly push the heels out to the side until the outside edge of each foot run parallel (the toes are facing forward in a straight line). At this point, allow the knees to bend as if sitting down. The height of the stance is about that of a normal sitting position.

Fig 57 Kiba Dachi.

Fig 58 Koko Hiza Kuzushi.

The posterior should not protrude. The body weight should be supported by the feet rather than the knees.

KOKO HIZA KUZUSHI

Tiger mouth, knee level. This is an unbalancing technique directed at the knee of the attacker's oncoming striking leg. While stepping into a right front stance, draw the left open hand across the abdomen to the right side of the body and slightly forward. At the same time, drive the right open hand downward to a low-level blocking position. The intention here is to drive under the attacker's leg with the left hand and, while holding the leg, drive downward to the knee with the right hand.

KOKUTSU DACHI

Back bent leg stance. See diagram for positioning the feet. The body is turned sideways but the head stills looks forward; the body weight is moved over the back leg rather than the front and the heels are in alignment. The front foot is facing forward and the rear foot is angled at 90 degrees. Keep the body upright.

KOSA DACHI

Crossed stance. Stepping with the right leg forward in stance, draw the left foot toward and to the outside edge of the right foot. The right foot should be firmly planted, and the ball of the left foot should be

Fig 59 Kokutsu Dachi.

touching the floor with the heel raised and the foot angled toward the outside edge of the right foot.

KOSA UKE

Crossed block. Raise the right fist to the left shoulder with the back of the fist to the face and the elbow close to the chest. Drive forward in a diagonal line from left to right until the fist is level with the right shoulder and in line with the right knee. The arm should be bent at the elbow in a 'V' shape. When this point is reached, allow the fist to turn clockwise until the palm is facing upward. At the same time, raise the left fist

Fig 60 Kosa Dachi.

Fig 61 Kosa Uke.

to the right shoulder, palm to the side of the face. Drive the back of the fist down to a low-level blocking position. When this point is reached, allow the fist to turn clockwise so the palm is facing downward.

KOSHI GAMAE

Hip posture. Draw the left fist to the left hip with the fingers facing upward. The little finger edge of the forearm should be resting against the lower left ribs. Maintain this left arm position and draw the right fist to the left fist so the little finger edge of the right fist is touching the upward facing fingers of the left hand.

MAE ENPI ZUKI

See *Mae Enpi*.

MAE ENPI

Front elbow. This is an elbow strike used to defend against attack from the front, and is used here to strike the palm of the left hand.

MAE GERI

Front kick. Assume a left front stance. Drive upward with the right knee to about abdomen or chest height, and, pivoting at

Fig 62 Koshi Gamae.

Fig 63 Mae Enpi.

Fig 64 Mae Geri.

Fig 65 Manji Gamae.

the knee, drive forward and upward using the ball of the foot to make the strike.

MANJI GAMAE

Swastika posture. Allow the arms to cross parallel to each other by the solar plexus, then raise the left arm up to the left side of the body in a high-level block in an 'L' shape, and lower the right arm into a right low-level block. The left arm is angled to 90 degrees with the fingers of the fist facing to the back of the head; the attention is focused on the right low-level block.

MANJI UKE

Swastika posture. The position for this is the same as for *Manji Gamae,* but with the intention of blocking.

MAWASHI KAKE UKE

Round suspend block. Extend both arms out to the front. The left hand should be level with the left shoulder with the palm directed downward. The right hand should be level with the lower ribs on the right side of the body with the palm directed upward. When this position is reached, rotate both open hands in a clockwise direction, drawing the right open hand to the right hip with the fingers directed downward, and the left open hand close to the left side of the upper chest with the fingers directed upward.

Fig 67 Mawashi Kake Uke (2)

Fig 66 Mawashi Kake Uke (1)

Fig 68 Mawashi Kake Uke (3)

MIKAZUKI GERI

Crescent moon kick. Standing in a left front stance, drive the right foot around in an arc to a front low-, middle- or high-level striking position. Use the sole of the foot to make the block.

MIZUNAGARE NO KAMAE

Water flowing posture. This refers to the positioning of the right or left arm across the chest which is angled down slightly as in flowing water. The fist is closed and the thumb edge of the fist is directed toward the chest. The fingers of the fist should be in line with the ribs and about six inches away from the chest.

Fig 70 Morote Enshin Haito Barai.

MOROTE ENSHIN HAITO BARAI

Two hand centrifugal sword sweep. Extend both open hands out to high level to the left side of the body. Rotate the arms in a large clockwise circular motion up above head height out to the right of the body and finally out to the left side of the body at middle level. The palms of the hands should be directed upward and the thumbs tucked in across the palms.

MOROTE GEDAN IPPON NUKITE

Two hand, low level, one pierce hand. Assuming a right foot cat stance, raise the thumb edge of each hand to a middle-level blocking position with the index fingers

Fig 69 Mikazuki Geri.

Fig 71 Morote Gedan Ippon Nukite.

Fig 72 Morote Gedan Shuto Uke.

MOROTE HAIWAN UKE

Two hand back arm block. Assuming a left back stance, lower both arms down to low level and slightly to the rear. Driving in an upward arc, raise the left arm out to the front in an 'L' shape; the upper arm should be in line with the shoulder, the forearm

extended and pointing downward. Make a short sliding motion (*Yori Ashi*) and drive both fingers downward in a low-level striking action.

MOROTE GEDAN SHUTO UKE

Two hand low-level sword hand block. Step into a left back stance. Draw both open hands out to the rear, then, sweeping outward and around in an arc, drive both open hands down to a low-level blocking position. The left hand palm is facing downward, and the right hand palm is directed upward, that is the little finger edges are used to make the block.

Fig 73 Morote Haiwan Uke.

vertical and the fingers of the fist should be directed to the right. At the same time, raise the right arm so the back of the right fist is resting close to the temple and the elbow is directed out to the rear.

MOROTE JO TSUKI DASHI

Two hands, Jo, thrusting, counter. This technique involves thrusting both open hand forward to block against a Jo Staff. In this instance the staff is vertical so the left hand is at high level and the right hand is at low level.

MOROTE JO UKE

Two hand Jo Staff block. The posture for this is the same as *Morote Jo Tsuki Dashi*, but with the intention of taking the Jo Staff from an opponent.

MOROTE KAISHU GEDAN UKE

Two hands, open hand, low level, block. Assume a horse riding *Kiba Dachi* stance. Looking to the left extend both open hands to a low level position to the right of the body. To make the block, rotate both open hands forward and upward in a complete circle and finish the block at a low level position to the front of the body.

MOROTE KEITO UKE

Two hand chicken head block. Assuming a right foot cat stance, extend both arms out to either side of the body to low-level positions, and sweep upward with the thumb edges of the hands to a middle-level blocking position with the index fingers extended.

Fig 74 Morote Jo Uke.

Fig 75 Morote Keito Uke.

89

MOROTE UKE

Two hand block. This block is very similar to *Ude Uke*. Raise the right fist to the left shoulder with the back of the fist to the face and the elbow close to the chest. Drive forward in a diagonal line from left to right until the fist is level with the right shoulder. The arm should be bent at the elbow in a 'V' shape. When this point is reached, allow the fist to turn clockwise until the palm is facing upward. While performing this action, draw the left fist to the right elbow, to the side of and just behind the elbow joint, with the fingers of the left fist directed upward. The left fist is intended to support the right blocking arm.

Fig 76 Morote Koko Uke.

Fig 77 Morote Uke.

MOROTE KOKO UKE

Assume a left back stance. Extend the right open hand to a middle-level blocking position and the left open hand to a high-level blocking position as if blocking against a Bo Staff. The left forearm is slightly above head height, and the fingers of the left hand are angled downward slightly. The upper right arm is tucked into the ribs, the forearm is horizontal, and the palm of the open hand is directed forward with the fingers angled downward.

Fig 78 Morote Zuki.

Fig 79 Muso Gamae.

MOROTE ZUKI

Two hand strike. Draw both fists to the right hip with the fingers facing upward. Drive both fists out to the left side of the body. The right arm should be positioned across the chest and in line with the left shoulder, and the left arm should be extended with the palm of the fist directed downward.

MOTO DACHI

Resulting stance. This is a resulting stance of twisting the body while performing a technique. In this instance it resembles a short Zenkutsu Dachi.

MUSO GAMAE

Nil posture. Step forward with the right foot into a straddle stance. Raise the left arm to a high-level blocking position with the left forearm slightly above and in front of the forehead, with the fingers of the fist facing forward. At the same time, lower the right arm to a low-level blocking position.

MUSO UKE

Only one block. Draw the forearms upward close together and close to the face.

91

Fig 81 Nagashi Uke.

Fig 80 Muso Uke.

The fingers of the fists are directed toward the head, and the little gap between the wrists is used to see through.

NAGASHI UKE

Sweeping block. Assume a left back stance, and extend the left arm, with the fist closed and the fingers directed downward, to a middle-level position. Sweep upward toward the right side of the face with the left forearm. As the arm is drawn upward, the fist turns so that the fingers of the fist are directed toward the face.

NAGASHI UKE

Sweeping block. Extend the left fist out to the front of the body to a low-level blocking position. Sweep the right arm out to the right side of the body and slightly to the rear, with the forearm vertically aligned, creating an 'L' shape, and the fingers of the right hand directed toward the left side of the body.

NAIWAN KAKIWAKE

Forearm wedging block. Move the fists across the body until they cross at the solar plexus. The inside of the right forearm should be just in front of the outside of the left forearm and the fingers of the fists should be facing away to either side of the

Fig 82 Nagashi Uke.

body. Continue moving the arms upward and forward and allow them to separate at about shoulder height. Keep the elbows bent and close to the chest. Bring the right fist in line with the right shoulder and the left fist in line with the left shoulder. At this point, allow the fists to turn, the right in an anti-clockwise direction and the left in a clockwise direction, until the palms are directed toward the body.

NAIWAN SUKUI NAGE

Hit or strike arm scooping throw. Draw the left foot to the right foot in a standing position, and, bending at the knees, make a large, low scooping circle with the right arm, from the left to the right side of the body. The fingers of the right fist are directed upward, as if making a hammer fist strike.

Fig 83 Naiwan Kakiwake.

Fig 84 Naiwan Suki Nage.

NAKADAKA IPPON KEN

Inside, middle, or one fist. Standing in a right front stance, extend the arms to the front, then sweep around with both fists to the rear of the body at middle-level striking positions. The gap between the fists should be about body width, and the knuckles are directed inward with the second finger knuckle protruding. This technique can also be performed by extending both arms to the rear, and driving forward with the fists to middle level. Again, the gap between the fists should be about body width, and the knuckles are directed inward with the second finger knuckle protruding

Fig 86 Neko Ashi Dachi.

NEKO ASHI DACHI

Cat leg stance. This stance is sometimes referred to as the cat stance, because it resembles a cat about to pounce on its prey. See diagram for positioning the feet. The body weight is supported by the right leg. Bend the right knee slightly. Resting on the ball of the right foot, turn the raised heel toward the instep of the left foot. The right toes should now be directed forward and the heel of the right foot directed toward the left instep. Remember to keep the body upright.

Fig 85 Nakadaka Ippon Ken.

Fig 87 Nihon Nukite.

Fig 88 Oi Zuki.

NIHON NUKITE

Two pierce hand. While stepping into a right front stance, draw the left fist to the left hip, and drive forward with the right hand to high-level. The first two fingers of the right hand are extended in a 'V' shape, and the palm of the hand is directed downward.

OI ZUKI

Lounge punch. Step into a right front stance, draw the left fist to the left hip with the fingers directed upward, and drive forward with the right fist. The fist should drive forward with the fingers facing

upward and the elbow tucked into the body. As the striking fist goes forward the inside of the upper right arm should skim past the right side of the chest. At the end of the strike allow the fist to turn anti-clockwise in a semi-circle until the fingers are directed downward

OSAE UKE

Pressing block. Raise the right open hand forward and upward to a point about 12in in front of the left side of the face, palm facing to the right. Keep the elbow tucked into the chest. The arm should now be in a vertical 'V' shape with the fingers pointing upward. Pivoting on the elbow, allow the

95

Fig 90 Ryo Goshi Gamae.

Fig 89 Osae Uke.

left hand palm to lower until the fingertips are level with the right side of the chest and in line with the abdomen. The arm should be sloping down to the right slightly.

RYO GOSHI GAMAE

Both hands back hip posture. Standing in a horse riding stance, draw both fists back to the hips – the left fist to the left hip and the right fist to the right hip. The fingers of both fists are directed upward, and the elbows are tucked in to the body.

RYO KAISHU GAMAE

Both hands, open hands, posture. Rotate both arms in large circles – the right in an anti-clockwise direction and the left in a clockwise direction – out to the sides of the body up above head height, down past the body and out again to the sides. At this point the palms of the open hands are directed downward.

RYO WAN ZEMPO NOBASHI

Two arm forward direction stretch. Stand in an informal attention stance and drive forward with both arms parallel and the fingers of the fists directed downward.

Fig 91 Ryo Kaishu Gamae.

Fig 92 Ryo Wan Zempo Nobashi.

RYOKEN KOSHI GAMAE

Both fists hip posture. Draw both fists to the hips with the fingers directed away from the rear of the body and the elbows directed out to the left and right sides (akimbo).

RYOTE FUSE

Both hands face down. Assume a right front stance. Allow the body to drop forward and downward until the chest is close to the right knee. Extend both open hands down to the floor with the fingers directed forward.

RYOWAN GAMAE

Both arms posture. Rotate both arms in complete circles past the face and body, the left arm in a clockwise direction, and the

Fig 93 Ryoken Koshi Gamae.

Fig 94 Ryote Fuse.

Fig 96 Ryowan Uchi Uke.

Fig 95 Ryowan Gamae.

RYOWAN UCHI UKE

Both arms striking block. The action for this technique is the same as for *Kakiwake Uchi*, with the palms of the fists directed toward the face (the outer forearms make the blocking action).

RYUSUI NO KAMAE

Flowing water. The position for this technique is the same as for *Mizunagare No Kamae*, but with the hand open and the palm facing downward.

RYUSUI ZUKI

Flowing water strike. This could be a follow-on from *Ryusui No Kamae*. In a left back stance assume the *Ryusui No Kamae* posture, then drive the right fist forward under the left open hand to middle level.

right arm in an anti-clockwise direction. The arms should cross by the face and drive downward and outward until they are level with the hips on either side of the body. The hands are closed with the palms facing toward the hips and there should be about a 12in space between palm and hip.

Fig 97 Ryusui No Kamae.

SAGI ASHI DACHI

Heron leg stance. From a right front stance, draw the left foot around to the right knee, allowing the body to turn sideways to the right. The sole of the left foot should be directed toward the right knee.

Fig 98 Ryusui Zuki.

Fig 99 Sagi Ashi Dachi.

Fig 100 Sanchin Dachi.

Fig 101 Sankaku Tobi.

SANCHIN DACHI

Three battle stance. Very similar to *Hangetsu Dachi,* but shorter in stance.

SANKAKU TOBI

Three corner jump. Step into a right front stance. While performing a complete circle, jump into the air and land once more into a right front stance. In the kata *Meikyo,* an Enpi strike is made halfway through the jump, hence three corners.

SEIRYUTO UCHI

Forward thrusting hit or strike. Standing in a cat stance, draw both open hands

Fig 102 Seiryuto Uchi.

toward the upper abdomen. Sliding forward slightly (*Yori Ashi*), drive both palm heels downward to a low-level blocking position. The palms should be angled outward.

SENPU TOBI GERI

Whirlwind fly kick. This involves making one complete turn plus one quarter turn while jumping into the air. In the kata *Unsu*, it also involves making a kicking action while making the jump.

Fig 104 Shaho Sashi Ashi.

Fig 103 Senpu Tobi Geri.

SHAHO SASHI ASHI

Diagonal balance foot/leg. This is a diagonal stepping action made by stepping with one foot over the other.

SHIHON NUKITE

Pierce hand. This is very often accompanied by a pressing block. Step into a right front stance, and at the same time drive forward with the right open hand with the thumb edge directed upward and the palm directed to the left. The thumb and the fingers should be pressed together, and the strike is made at middle level.

SHIZENTAI

Natural posture. This is not really a stance, but more of a relaxed and natural body condition while standing.

Fig 105 Shihon Nukite.

Fig 106 Shizentai.

SHUTO DOJI UKE

Sword hand, at the same time, hit or strike. Assume a right front stance, then drive both open hands outward and around to the rear in an arc to high level. At this point the palms of the hands are angled downward.

Fig 107 Shuto Doji Uke.

SHUTO GEDAN BARAI

Knife hand low-level sweeping. Basically, this is the same as *Gedan Barai,* but with the hand open. Here the technique is performed in a very low form of *Kokutsu Dachi.* The right leg is forward, the body is low. The right open hand is level with and just above the right leg, and the left open hand is level with the solar plexus, with the little finger edge just touching the abdomen.

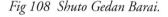

Fig 108 Shuto Gedan Barai.

Fig 109 Shuto Uke.

SHUTO UKE

Knife hand block. Stepping with the right foot forward in stance, draw the right open hand to the right shoulder with the palm to the face and the left elbow close to the solar plexus. Allow the arm to pivot at the elbow and drive forward with the thumb edge of the right hand in a diagonal line from right to left, until the hand is almost level with the right shoulder with the palm facing upward. When this point is reached, allow the hand to flip over so that the palm is now facing downward and the outer edge, or little finger edge, of the hand makes the strike. Do not allow the elbow to point away from the body; keep the triceps in line with the side of the chest with a gap of about 6in. While performing this action draw the left open hand back to the body with the palm facing upward and the edge of the hand resting on the solar plexus. The hands should be straight with the fingers pressed together.

SOCHIN DACHI

Battle stance. This is similar to *Zenkutsu Dachi*, but with the front foot angled inward and the back leg bent. The body weight is evenly distributed.

Fig 110 Sochin Dachi.

Fig 111 Soete Kake Dori.

SOETE KAKE DORI

Suspend hand catch. Assume a left front stance. Sweep the right open hand in front of the body and raise it to the left shoulder height with the palm facing upward. At the same time, allow the left open hand to rest on the right wrist. At this point allow the right hand to turn over so the palm is directed downward.

SOIHEI BO DORI

Horizontal or level stick catch. Assume a left back stance. Raise the right open hand so the back of the hand is in line with the temple and the fingers directed forward. The palm is angled upward and the elbow

Fig 112 Soihei Bo Dori.

pushed back toward the head. Keeping the left arm slightly bent, raise it to about middle level. The hand should be approximately in line with the left foot, the palm directed upward and the fingers directed forward. Both hands are slightly arched as if catching a stick or a Bo Staff. At this point, allow the right hand to turn over in a clockwise direction so that the palm is facing downward. At the same time, raise the left hand upward to about shoulder height.

SOKUMEN GEDAN BARAI

Side-facing low-level sweep. This is a *Gedan Barai* performed while facing sideways, often in horse riding stance; while in horse riding stance draw the right fist to the left shoulder, then drive it outward and downward to the right of the body to a low-level blocking position.

Fig 113 Sokumen Gedan Barai.

SOKUMEN GYAKU ZUKI

Side-facing reverse strike. While standing in horse riding stance, drive the right fist across the body to the left side to middle level. It is essential to try and keep the stance rather than turning the body to accommodate the strike.

Fig 114 Sokumen Gyaku Zuki.

SOKUMEN JODAN HAITO UKE

Side facing, high level, back sword hand block. Stepping into a left foot forward back stance (Kokutsu Dachi), raise the left open hand to high level with the arm in a 'L' shape. The back of the hand is used to make the block, and the arm should be in line with the left leg.

105

Fig 115 Sokumen Morote Zuki.

Fig 116 Sokumen Tate Enpi.

SOKUMEN MOROTE ZUKI

Side-facing two hand strike. While standing in horse riding stance, draw both fists to the left hip then drive them both out to the right side of the body to about middle level. At this point the fingers of both hands are directed downward.

SOKUMEN TATE ENPI

Side-facing vertical elbow. Standing in horse riding stance, drive the right fist upward and outward from the right hip to the right side of the body. Effectively, this draws the elbow upward vertically to strike, probably, under the chin. At the end of the technique the elbow is directed to the side and the forearm is horizontal.

SOKUMEN ZUKI

In this instance, the fist is driven across the chest to make a strike to the side.

SOTO UKE

Outside block. In the kata *Unsu,* this technique is used while standing on one leg (*Ippon Dachi*), and the block itself is very similar to *Uchi Komi*.

SUIHEI HIJI GAMAE

Horizontal or level elbow posture. Assume a posture and raise both fists upward to chest height so the thumb edges of the fists are in line with, and about 2in away from the nipples. The elbows are directed outward horizontally at either side of the body.

Fig 117 Sokumen Zuki.

Fig 119 Suihei Hiji Gamae.

Fig 118 Soto Uke.

TAI OTOSHI

Body dropping. This is literally dropping the body, and in the kata *Unsu* the body is dropped to the floor on one side.

TATE ENPI

Vertical elbow. Standing in a right front stance, drive the right fist from the right hip upward and past the right side of the face. Effectively, this draws the elbow upward vertically to strike, probably, under the chin. At the end of the technique the elbow is directed forward and the forearm is horizontal.

Fig 120   Tai Otoshi.

Fig 122   Tate Enpi Zuki.

Fig 121   Tate Enpi.

TATE ENPI ZUKI

Vertical elbow strike. Effectively this is the same as *Tate Enpi*, but with the intention of making strike.

TATE KEN GYAKU ZUKI

Vertical fist reverse strike. In the kata *Chinte*, this involves standing in a front stance and striking upward to the opposite extended open hand.

Fig 123 Tate Ken Gyaku Zuki.

TATE SHUTO UKE

Vertical sword hand block. This is an open hand block which scoops around from one side of the body to the other. For example, standing in a horse riding stance, raise the right hand to the left shoulder and push outward and around to the right side. Throughout the action the palm of the open hand is directed outward, and the fingers directed upward.

TATE URAKEN UCHI

Vertical back fist hit or strike. Standing in a front stance, raise the right fist above the head, then drive the back of the fist forward and downward to about middle level. The aim of this technique is to use the knuckles of the fist to make the strike. At the end of this technique the fingers of the right hand should be angled upward.

Fig 124 Tate Shuto Uke.

Fig 125 Tate Uraken Uchi.

109

Fig 126 Teisho Awaze Zuki.

Fig 127 Teisho Tate Hasami Uchi.

TEISHO AWAZE ZUKI

Palm heel, join, strike. Standing in a left front stance, draw both palm heels to the hips and drive forward, the left at low level, the right at high level. At this point both palm heels are directed forward, the fingers of the left hand are directed downward, and the fingers of the right hand are directed upward.

TEISHO TATE HASAMI UCHI

Palm heel vertical attack on both sides, hit or strike. Assume a left front stance. Extend the left arm forward so that the palm is directed forward and the fingers are directed upward. Draw the right wrist upward to the left wrist. The fingers of the right hand should be directed downward and the palm forward.

TEISHO UCHI

Palm heel strike. The action for this technique is similar to *Teisho Uke,* but the palm heel is driven out to the side of the body in a striking action.

TEISHO UKE

Palm heel block. As the name suggests, this is a block using the palm heel of the hand. It can be made in several ways and directions. When directed upward, the palm would be facing forward and the fingers directed upward. When directed to a low level, the palm would be facing forward and the fingers directed downward. Likewise, the hand position would be the same when directed to the side at low or high level.

Fig 128 Teisho Uchi.

Fig 130 Tenshin Tobi Gaeshi.

Fig 129 Teisho Uke.

TENSHIN TOBI GAESHI

Turning, jumping, return. This involves jumping while turning in a complete circle and returning to the start of the posture. For example, stand in a right back stance and a right sword hand posture (*Shuto Uke*). From this position turn and jump high in the air, and land in a right back stance performing a right sword hand block.

TETTSUI UCHI

Hammer fist strike. Raise the right fist to the left shoulder with the fingers to the right side of the face. Allow the upper body to turn slightly to the left. Drive the back of the fist forward in an arc and out to the right side of the body to middle level. When the arm is almost extended, allow the fist to turn clockwise so the little finger edge of the fist is facing to the rear.

TETTSUI UKE

Hammer fist block. As for *Tettsui Uchi*, but with the intention of blocking rather than striking.

Fig 131 Tettsui Uchi.

TOBI ASHI BARAI

Flying foot sweep. Standing in a right front stance, turn the head to face the rear and raise the right extended hand to the rear at about head height. While leaping into the air, sweep the left hand with the right foot,

Fig 132 Tobi Ashi Barai.

and, making a complete circle, land in a right front stance.

TOBI USHIRO GERI

Flying back kick. The movement for this technique is similar to *Tobi Ashi Barai*, except that the left hand is not swept by the right foot, rather the right foot performs a back kick while in flight and turning in a complete circle.

TSUKAMI DORI

Catch hold of, catch. Assume a left front stance. Sweep the right open hand in front of the body and raise it to left shoulder height with the palm facing upward. At the same time, allow the left open hand to rest on the right wrist. At this point, allow the right hand to turn over so the palm is directed downward.

Fig 133 Tobi Ushiro Geri.

Fig 135 Tsuru Ashi Dachi.

Fig 134 Tsukami Dori.

TSURU ASHI DACHI

Crane leg stance. Stand on the left leg with the knee slightly bent. Draw the right foot to just behind the left knee so that the top of the foot is resting in the hollow behind the left knee.

UCHI KOMI

Hit or strike, in. Raise the right fist above head height. Step forward into a right front stance, and at the same time drive downward and across the body to the left side. The right fist should be in line with the left shoulder and the fingers of the right fist

113

Fig 136 Uchi Komi.

Fig 137 Uchi Uke.

directed upward. The gap between the left shoulder and the right fist should be about the same length as the forearm.

UCHI UKE

Hit or strike, block. Step into a right front stance. Raise the right fist to the left shoulder with the back of the fist to the face and the elbow close to the chest. Drive forward in a diagonal line from left to right until the fist is level with the right shoulder and in line with the right knee. The arm should be bent at the elbow in a 'V' shape. When this point is reached, allow the fist to turn clockwise until the palm is facing upward.

UDE UKE

See *Uchi Uke*.

URA ASHIGAKE

Back leg suspend. From any stance, turn the body and the head to face the rear. Sweep the left foot around to the rear in an arc and confirm in the stance. The intention here is to catch the leg or foot of an oncoming attacker and frustrate the attack.

URAKEN UCHI

Back fist. This is often used in combination with *Yoko Geri Keage*: drive out to the side with the back of the fist, and when the arm is extended at head height allow the wrist to flex. The arm and wrist should make a whipping action as the strike is made, that is a fast recoiling action with the knuckles making contact rather than the back of the hand. Alternatively, drive forward, as

Fig 138 Ura Ashigake.

shown, using the same whipping action to strike the attacker at middle level.

USHIRO NAKADAKA IPPON KEN

Back inside/middle/one true fist. Extend both arms out to the front at middle level. The hands are closed to form a fist with the second finger knuckle protruding. Drive outward to the sides then around to the rear to strike with both fists at middle level. Once the strike is made the second finger knuckles are directed toward each other.

Fig 139 Uraken Uchi.

Fig 140 Ushiro Nakadaka Ippon Ken.

Fig 141 Ushiro Teisho Barai.

Fig 142 Ushiro Tettsui Hasami Uchi.

USHIRO TEISHO BARAI

Back palm heel sweep. Assume a right front stance. Sweep around to the rear with the left hand. At the end of the sweep the fingers of the right hand are directed downward with the palm heel of the right hand thrusting to the rear.

USHIRO TETTSUI HASAMI UCHI

Back, iron hammer, attack/both sides, hit/strike. Extend both arms to the front. Close the hands to form a fist with the fingers directed downward. Drive out to the sides of the body and around to the rear. The strike is made using the little finger edge of each hand and the fingers remain directed downward.

WASHITE AGE UCHI

Eagle hand rising, hit or strike. Press the first two fingers and thumb of the right hand together to form a point. The strike is made by driving upward, probably under the upper arm of the attacker, to strike at the nerve points.

WASHITE OTOSHI UCHI

Eagle hand dropping, hit or strike. This is a very similar technique to that of *Washite Age Uchi*, but with the emphasis on a downward or dropping action rather than a

Fig 143 Washite Age Uchi.

rising action. For example, press the first two fingers and thumb of the right hand together to form a point. The strike is made by driving or dropping downward, probably on to the upper arm of the attacker, to strike at the nerve points.

YAMA ZUKI

Mountain punch. Step with the right foot into a front stance. Drive the right arm forward to make a middle-level punch and, at the same time, drive the left fist over the head to make a high-level punch. At the end of this strike the fists should be in vertical alignment.

Fig 144 Washite Otoshi Uchi.

Fig 145 Yama Zuki.

YOKO GERI KEAGE

Side kick snapping. Raise the right foot to the height of the left knee, and drive the right foot out to the side to about waist height, driving with the hips. The outer edge of the right foot should make contact.

Fig 147 Yoko Geri Kekomi.

Fig 146 Yoko Geri Keage.

YOKO GERI KEKOMI

Sideways kick, crowded. Step into a horse riding stance. Raise the left knee and drive out to the side of the body with the heel of the right foot. Power is added to the strike by allowing the hip to twist as the strike is made.

YOKO UDE HASAMI

Side arm, both sides. This is a trapping block. Standing in a horse riding stance,

Fig 148 Yoko Ude Hasami.

drive the left arm upward from a low-level position, and the right arm downward from a high-level position. The inside of the right arm comes together with the outside of the left arm.

YORI ASHI

Sliding foot. This is simply a little sliding movement and may be performed in any stance. For this example step into a horse riding stance and, by lifting the weight of the right foot, slide to the right about 5 or 6in, then allow the left foot to move an equal distance in the same direction.

Fig 150 Yumi Zuki.

Fig 149 Yori Ashi.

YUMI ZUKI

Bow strike. The action for this technique is rather like using a bow: pull back with the left arm and drive out to the side with the right arm.

ZENPO ENPI UCHI

Forward bent elbow hit or strike. Step into a left front stance. Keeping the right arm bent with the fist positioned at the hip, drive upward with the elbow, allowing the right fist to pass close to the right ear. This is often performed by striking the left open hand.

ZENKUTSU DACHI

Front bent leg stance. Front stance is rather like taking a long step forward with a few extra simple guidelines. Before making the

Fig 151 Zenpo Enpi Uchi.

Fig 152 Zenkutsu Dachi.

step forward, gauge the width of the shoulders from left to right. Using that measurement, imagine two equal parallel lines on the floor with that same shoulder width distance between them. Place the left foot on the left line and the right foot on the right line. Step along the left line with the left foot as far as you can without wobbling or falling and keep the body facing forward.

Allow the right foot to turn 35 degrees to the right and keep the left foot pointing forward. Keeping the feet firmly in place, move the body weight forward by bending the left knee until it is vertically level with the toes. Keep the sole of the right foot firmly planted on the floor and do not allow it to roll on to the inner edge. Keep the body upright.

Japanese Dictionary

Romaji	Kanji	Kata Names	Interpretation
Age Uke	上受	Heian Shodan	Rising block
Age Zuki	上突	Enpi	Rising thrust
Ashi Barai	足払	Bassai Sho	Foot Sweep
Awaza Shuto Age Uke	合手刀上受	Chinte	Join, sword hand, rising, block
Awaza Teisho Zuki	合底掌突	Nijushiho	Join, palm heel, strike
Awaza Zuki	合突	Nijushiho	Join, strike
Bassai Dai	找塞大		Draw out the enemy, fortress, large
Bassai Sho	找塞小		Penetrate or block, fortress, small
Bo Dori Tsuki Otoshi	棒捕臭落	Kanku Sho	Stick, catch, thrust, dropping
Bo Uke	棒受	Kanku Sho	Bo, catch
Chinte	珍手		Rare or uncommon, hand
Chudan Zuki	中段突	Heian Shodan	Middle level, strike
Doji Fumikomi	同時踏込	Jion	At the same time, stamping
Doji Haito Uchi	同時背刀打	Bassai Sho	At the same time, back sword, hit or strike
Doji Uke	同時受	Bassai Sho	At the same time, hit or strike
Doji Ushiro Gedan Uke	同時後下段受	Gojushiho Sho	At the same time, back, low level, block
Enpi	猿臂	Heian Sandan	Elbow, or long arm.
Enpi	燕飛		Swallow (bird) flying
Enpi Uchi	猿臂打	Sochin	Elbow, or long arm like a monkey, hit or strike
Fudo Dachi	不動立	Wankan	Steadfast, stance
Fumikomi	踏込	Heian Sandan	Stamping in
Gankaku	岩鶴		Rock crane
Gankaku Gamae	岩鶴構	Gankaku	Rock, crane, posture
Gedan Barai	下段払	Heian Shodan	Low level, sweep
Gedan Gamae	下段構	Kanku Dai	Low level, posture
Gedan Shuto Uchi	下段手刀打	Gojushiho Sho	Low level, sword hand, hit or strike
Goju shi ho Dai	五十四歩大		Fifty four steps, large
Goju shi ho Sho	五十四歩小		Fifty four steps, small
Gyaku Hanmi	逆半身	Heian Nidan	Reverse, to one side of the body or half the body
Gyaku Zuki	逆突	Heian Godan	Reverse, strike
Gyaku te Dori	逆手捕	Gankaku	Reverse hand, catch

Romaji	Kanji	Kata Names	Interpretation
Haimen Hasami Uchi	背面狭打	Chinte	Back, both sides, hit or strike
Haishu Age Uke	背手上受	Nijushiho	Back hand, rising, receive / block
Haishu Awaze Uke	背手合受	Gankaku	Back hand, join, block
Haishu Juji Uke	背手十字受	Heian Godan	Back hand, cross, block
Haishu Uke	背手受	Kanku Sho	Back hand, block
Haito Ippon Ken	背刀一本拳	Hangetsu	Back sword, one, fist
Haito Kakiwake.	背刀掻分	Gankaku	Back sword, dividing
Haito Sukui Nage	背刀掬投	Bassai Sho	Back sword, scooping, throw
Haito Uke	背刀受	Jitte	Back sword, block
Haiwan Uke	背腕受	Heian Nidan	Back arm, block
Hangetsu	半月		Half moon
Hangetsu Dachi	半月立	Hangetsu	Half moon, stance
Hanmi Sashi Ashi	半身差足	Hangetsu	One side of the body or half the body, on tiptoe
Hasami Uchi	狭打	Gojushiho Dai	Both sides, hit or strike
Heian Godan	平安五段		Peaceful calm, beginning level five
Heian Nidan	平安二段		Peaceful calm, beginning level two
Heian Sandan	平安三段		Peaceful calm, beginning level three
Heian Shodan	平安初段		Peaceful calm, beginning level one
Heian Yondan	平安四段		Peaceful calm, beginning level four
Heiko Tate Zuki	平行縦突	Gojushiho Sho	Parallel, vertical, strike
Heiko Ura Zuki	平行裏突	Bassai Sho	Parallel, back, punch
Heisoku Dachi	閉促立	Heian Sandan	Close, foot, stand
Hiji Barai	肘払	Gankaku	Arm, sweep
Hineri Kaeshi	捻返	Kanku Sho	Twist, return
Hirate Osae Uke	平手押受	Kanku Sho	Open hand i.e. palm, pressing, block
Hiza Gamae	膝構	Kanku Dai	Knee, posture
Hiza Uchi	膝打	Heian Yodan	Knee, hit or strike
Ippon Ken Furi Otoshi	一本拳振落	Chinte	One, fist, swing, dropping
Ippon Ken Gyaku Furi Otoshi	一本拳逆振落	Chinte	One, fist, reverse, swing, dropping
Ippon Nukite	一本貫手	Unsu	One, pierce, hand
Jiai No Kamae	慈愛の構	Jion	Benevolence, posture
Jin	慈落		Charity, assistance
Jion	慈恩		Mercy, kindness
Jitte	十手		Ten hand
Jo Kuzami	杖摑	Meikyo	Stick, to grasp
Jodan Morote Uke	上段諸手受	Jion	High level, two hand, block
Jodan Shuto Uchi	上段手刀打	Heian Yodan	High level, knife hand, hit or strike
Joho Kaiten Tobi	上方回転飛	Enpi	Above direction, spin, jump or fly

Romaji	Kanji	Kata Names	Interpretation
Joshin Gamae	淨心構	Meikyo	Clean pure, posture
Juji Uke	十字受	Heian Yodan	Cross, block
Jun Zuki	順突	Hangetsu	Turn, strike
Kaeshi Dori	返捕	Bassai Dai	Return, catch
Kaeshi Dori	返捕	Bassai Sho	Half, return, catch
Kagi Gamae	鍵構	Heian Godan	Key, posture
Kagi Zuki	鍵突	Tekki Shodan	Key, strike
Kaishu Haiwan Uke	開手背腕受	Heian Yodan	Open hand, back arm, block
Kaishu Juji Uke	開手十字受	Gankaku	Open hand crossed block
Kaishu Kosa Uke	開手交叉受	Gojushiho Dai	Open hand crossed block
Kaishu Ryowan Gamae	開手両腕構	Hangetsu	Open hand, both arms, posture
Kaishu Yama Gamae	開手山構	Hangetsu	Open hand, mountain, posture
Kaiun No Te	開雲の手	Unsu	Open, cloud, hand
Kake Dori	掛捕	Hangetsu	Suspend, catch
Kakiwake Uke	搔分受	Heian Yodan	Wedging, block or catch
Kami Zukami	髪掴	Enpi	Hair (on head), grasp hold of
Kanku Dai	観空大		Look at sky (large)
Kanku Dai Gamae	観空大構	Kanku Dai	Look at sky, large, posture
Kanku Sho	観空小		Look at sky (small)
Kasei Geri	下勢蹴	Unsu	Low force, kick
Kasui Ken	火水拳	Kanku Sho	Fire, water, fist
Kata Hiza Dachi	片膝立	Gankaku	One, knee, stand
Kataashi Dachi	片足立	Kanku Dai	One, foot, stand
Keito Uke	鶏頭受	Gojushiho Sho	Chicken head, block
Keito Uke	鶏頭受	Unsu	Chicken head, block
Kesage	蹴下	Bassai Dai	Kick down
Kiba Dachi	騎馬立	Heian Sandan	Horse riding, stand
Kin Geri	験蹴	Tekki Nidan	Testes, kick
Koho Tsuki Age	後方突上	Heian Godan	Back, thrust, rising
Koko Hiza Kuzushi	虎口膝崩	Nijushiho	Tiger mouth, knee, break or destroy
Koko Morote Uke	虎口諸手受	Gojushiho Sho	Tiger mouth, two hands, block
Kokutsu Dachi	後屈立	Heian Nidan	Back, bent, stand
Kosa Dachi	交叉立	Tekki Shodan	Cross, stand
Kosa Uke	交叉受	Heian Sandan	Cross, block
Koshi Gamae	腰構	Heian Nidan	Hip, posture
Mae Enpi	前猿臂	Kanku Dai	Forward, elbow
Mae Geri	前蹴	Heian Nidan	Front, kick
Manji Gamae	卍構	Heian Godan	Swastika, stance
Manji Uke	卍受	Heian Godan	Swastika, block

Romaji	Kanji	Kata Names	Interpretation
Mawashi Geri	回蹴		Turn or spin, kick
Mawashi Kake Uke	回掛受	Nijushiho	Round, suspend, block
Meikyo	明鏡		Clear mirror
Mikazuki Geri	三日月蹴	Heian Godan	Crescent moon, kick
Mizunagare No Kamae	水渓の構	Tekki Sandan	Water, flow, posture
Morote Enshin Haito Barai	諸手遠心背刀払	Chinte	Two hand, centrifugal, sword, sweep
Morote Gedan Ippon Nukite	諸手下段一本貫手	Gojushiho Sho	Two hand, Gedan, one, pierce hand
Morote Gedan Shuto Uke	諸手下段刀受	Gankaku	Two hand, low level knife hand, block
Morote Gedan Uke	諸手下段受	Gankaku	Two hand, low level, block
Morote Haiwan Uke	諸手背腕受	Meikyo	Two hand, back arm, block
Morote Hiki Otoshi	諸手引落	Bassai Sho	Two hand, pull, dropping
Morote Jo Tsuki Dashi	諸手杖突出	Jitte	Two hands, stick, thrust out
Morote Jo Uke	諸手杖受	Meikyo	Two hands, Jo, block,
Morote Kaishu Gedan Uke	諸手開手下段受	Gojushiho Dai	Two hand, open hand, low level, block
Morote Kaishu Gedan Uke	諸手開手下段受	Gojushiho Sho	Two hand, open hand, low level, block
Morote Keito Uke	諸手鶏頭受	Gojushiho Dai	Two hand, chicken head, block
Morote Koko Dori	諸手虎口捕	Jitte	Two hands, tiger mouth, catch
Morote Koko Gamae	諸手虎口構	Enpi	Two hands, tiger mouth, posture
Morote Koko Uke	諸手虎口受	Bassai Sho	Two hand, tiger mouth, block
Morote Kubi Osae	諸手首押	Heian Yodan	Two hand, Neck, pressing
Morote Uke	諸手受	Heian Nidan	Two hand, blocks
Morote Yoko Ken Ate	諸手横拳当	Hangetsu	Two hands, side, fist, hit
Morote Zuki	諸手突	Tekki Shodan	Two hand, strikes
Moto Dachi	基立	Kanku Dai	Basic, stance
Muso Gamae	無双構	Sochin	Nil, posture
Muso Uke	無双受	Nijushiho	Only one, block
Nagashi Uke	流受	Heian Godan	Sweeping, block
Naiwan Kakiwake	内腕搔分	Gankaku	Hit or strike arm, wedging
Naiwan Sukui Nage	内腕掬投	Chinte	Hit or strike arm, scooping, throw
Nakadaka Ippon Ken	中高一本拳	Chinte	Inside or middle, one, fist
Nami Ashi	波足	Tekki Shodan	Wave, foot
Neko Ashi Dachi	猫足立	Gojushiho Dai	Cat, foot, stance
Nidan Geri	二段蹴	Gankaku	Two level, kick
Nihon Nukite	二本貫手	Chinte	Two, pierce hand
Nijushiho	二十四歩		Twenty four steps
Nikeito Gamae	二鶏頭構	Unsu	Two chicken, head, posture
Ofuri Kosa Barai	大振交叉払	Nijushiho	Large wave, cross, sweep
Oi Zuki	追突	Heian Shodan	Pursuing, strike
Osae Uke	押受	Heian Sandan	Pressing, block

Romaji	Kanji	Kata Names	Interpretation
Otoshi Doji Fumikomi	落同時踏込	Gojushiho Sho	Dropping, at the same time, stamping
Otoshi Zuki	落突	Kanku Dai	Dropping, strike
Renoji Dachi	しの字立	Heian Godan	Standing
Ryo Hiji Harai Age	両肘払上	Tekki Nidan	Two, elbows, sweeping, upward
Ryo Koshi Gamae	両腰横	Meikyo	Both hands, back hip, posture
Ryo Ude Mawashi Uke	両腕回受	Kanku Dai	Two, arm, round, block
Ryo Wan Zempo Nobashi	両腕前方伸	Gojushiho Dai	Two, arm, forward direction, stretch
Ryoken Koshi Gamae	両拳腰横	Heian Sandan	Two, hip, posture
Ryote Fuse	両手伏	Kanku Dai	Two hands, down
Ryowan Gamae	両腕横	Meikyo	Two arm, posture
Ryowan Gedan Kakiwake	両腕下段掻分	Jion	Two arm, low level, Wedging
Ryowan Kaishu Gamae	両腕開手横	Gojushiho Dai	Two arm, open hand, posture
Ryowan Uchi Uke	両腕打内	Meikyo	Two arm, hit or strike, block
Ryusui No Kamae	渓水の構	Tekki Sandan	Flowing water, posture
Ryusui Zuki	渓水突	Nijushiho	Flowing water, strike
Sagi Ashi Dachi	鷺足立	Jitte	Heron, leg, stance
Sanchin Dachi	三戦立	Nijushiho	Three battle, stance
Sankaku Tobi	三角飛	Meikyo	Three corner, jump
Sashi Ashi	差足	Wankan	Tiptoe
Seiryuto Uchi	青竜刀打	Gojushiho Dai	Forward thrusting, hit or strike
Sempu Tobi Geri	旋風飛蹴	Unsu	Whirlwind, fly, kick
Shaho Sashi Ashi	斜方差足	Wankan	Diagonal, balance, foot/leg
Shihon Nukite Zuki	四本貫手突	Heian Nidan	Four, spear hand, strike
Shizentai	自然体	Heian Shodan	Natural posture
Shuto Gedan Barai	手刀下段払	Heian Yodan	Knife hand, low level, sweep
Shuto Kakiwake	手刀掻分	Gankaku	Knife hand, wedging
Shuto Uke	手刀受	Heian Shodan	Knife hand, block
Sochin	壮鎮		Strong or large, calm, quiet
Sochin Dachi	壮鎮立	Sochin	Battle, stance
Soesho Chudan Zuki	添掌中段突	Tekki Sandan	Palm, grasp, middle level, strike
Soesho Hikite	添掌引手	Tekki Sandan	Palm, pull, hand
Soesho Kaeshi Ude	添掌返腕	Tekki Sandan	Palm, return, arm
Soete Kake Dori	添手掛捕	Kanku Sho	Suspend hand, catch
Soete Koshi Gamae	添手腰横	Tekki Nidan	Suspend hand, hip, posture
Soete Mae Enpi	添手前猿臂	Tekki Nidan	Suspend hand, front, elbow
Soete Sokumen Uke	添手側面受	Tekki Nidan	Suspend hand, side facing, block
Sokumen Enpi	側面猿臂	Tekki Shodan	Side facing, elbow
Sokumen Gedan Barai	側面下段払	Nijushiho	Side facing, low level, sweep
Sokumen Jodan Haito Uke	側面上段背刀受	Unsu	Side face, high level, back sword, block

125

Romaji	Kanji	Kata Names	Interpretation
Sokumen Morote Zuki	側面諸手突	Bassai Sho	Side facing, two hand, strike
Sokumen Soete Uchi Ude Uke	側面添手内腕受	Tekki Nidan	Side facing, support, hit or strike, arm, block
Sokumen Soto Uke	側面外受	Nijushiho	Side facing, outside, block
Sokumen Tate Shuto Uke	側面縦手刀受	Tekki Nidan	Side facing, vertical, knife hand, block
Sokumen Uke	側面受	Tekki Shodan	Side facing, block
Sokumen Zuki	側面突	Gankaku	Side facing, strike
Soto Ude Uke	外腕受	Tekki Nidan	Outside, arm, block
Soto Uke	外受	Bassai Dai	Outside, block
Sowan Uchi Uke	双腕内受	Jion	Pair arms, hit or strike, block
Suihei Bo Dori	水平棒捕	Bassai Sho	Horizontal or level, stick, catch
Suihei Hiji Gamae	水平肘構	Gojushiho Sho	Horizontal or level, elbow, posture
Suihei Uke	水平受		Horizontal or level, block
Sukui Uke	掬受	Bassai Dai	Scooping, block
Tachi Hiza	立膝	Enpi	Knee, stance
Tai Otoshi	体落	Unsu	Body, dropping
Taikokyu Shodan	初呼吸初段		First breath, level one
Taikokyu Nidan	初呼吸二段		First breath, level two
Taikokyu Sandan	初呼吸三段		First breath, level three
Tate Enpi Uchi	縦猿臂打	Gankaku	Vertical, elbow, hit or strike
Tate Ken Gyaku Zuki	縦拳逆突	Chinte	Vertical, fist, reverse, strike
Tate Nukite	縦貫手	Gojushiho Sho	Vertical, pierce through, hand
Tate Shuto Uke	縦手刀受	Heian Sandan	Vertical, knife hand, block
Tate Uraken Uchi	縦裏拳打	Kanku Sho	Vertical, back fist, hit or strike
Teisho Awaza Gedan Uke	底掌合下段受	Hangetsu	Palm heel, join, low level, block
Teisho Awaza Zuki	底掌合突	Nijushiho	Palm heel, join, strike
Teisho Kosa Uke	底掌交叉受	Enpi	Palm heel, cross, block
Teisho Morote Uke	底掌諸手受	Jitte	Palm heel, two hand, block
Teisho Tate Hasami Uchi	底掌縦狭打	Unsu	Palm heel, vertical, attack on both sides
Teisho Uchi	底掌打	Jion	Palm heel, hit or strike
Teisho Uke	底掌受	Enpi	Palm heel, block
Tekki Nidan	鉄騎二段		Iron horse riding level two
Tekki Sandan	鉄騎三段		Iron horse riding level three
Tekki Shodan	鉄騎初段		Iron horse riding level one
Tekubi Kake Uke	手首掛受	Jitte	Wrist, suspend, block
Tenchi Haito Uchi	天地背刀打	Nijushiho	Heaven, back sword, hit or strike
Tenchi Kenseitai	天地拳制体	Unsu	Sky earth, fist control, body
Tenshin Tobi Gaeshi	転身飛返	Kanku Sho	Turning, jumping, return
Tettsui Hasami Uchi	鉄槌挟打	Bassai Dai	Iron hammer, trap, hit or strike

Romaji	Kanji	Kata Names	Interpretation
Tettsui Uchi	鉄槌打	Chinte	Iron hammer, hit or strike
Tettsui Uchi	鉄槌打	Heian Shodan	Iron hammer, hit or strike
Tobi Geri	飛蹴	Kanku Dai	Flying kick
Tobi Mae Geri	飛前蹴	Gankaku	Flying, front, kick
Tobi Ushiro Geri	飛後蹴	Kanku Sho	Flying, back, kick
Tsukami Uke	掴受	Jion	Grasp hold of, block
Tsuru Ashi Dachi	鶴足立	Gankaku	Crane, leg, stance
Uchi Komi	打込		Hit or strike, in
Uchi Uke	内受	Sochin	Hit or strike, block
Ude Soete	腕添手	Heian Nidan	Arm, supported hand
Ude Uke	腕受	Heian Nidan	Arm, block
Unsu	雲手		Cloud, Hand
Ura Ashi Gake	裏足掛	Bassai Sho	Back, leg, suspend
Ura Zuki	裏突	Heian Nidan	Back, punch
Uraken Gamae	裏拳構	Hangetsu	Back fist, posture
Uraken Uchi	裏拳打	Heian Nidan	Back fist, hit or strike
Ushiro Gedan Barai	後下段払	Enpi	Back, low level, sweep
Ushiro Geri	後蹴		Back, kick
Ushiro Nakadaka Ippon Ken	後中高一本拳		Back, inside/middle/ one, true, fist
Ushiro Teisho Barai	後底掌払	Unsu	Back, palm heel, sweep
Ushiro Tettsui Hasami Uchi	後鉄槌挟打	Gojushiho Sho	Back, iron hammer, attack/both sides, hit/strike
Wankan	王冠		Crown
Washite Age Uchi	鷲手上打	Gojushiho Sho	Eagle hand, rising, hit or strike
Washite Otoshi Uchi	鷲手落打	Gojushiho Sho	Eagle hand, dropping, hit or strike
Yama Kakiwake	山搔分	Jitte	Mountain, wedging
Yama Uke	山受	Jitte	Mountain, block
Yama Zuki	山突	Bassai Dai	Mountain, strike
Yoi	用意	All	Awareness, ready
Yoko Geri Kekomi	横蹴蹴込	Nijushiho	Sideways, kick, crowded
Yoko Keage	横蹴上	Heian Nidan	Sideways, kick up
Yoko Sashi Ashi	横差足	Tekki Nidan	Sideways, stepping on tiptoe
Yoko Tettsui Uchi	横鉄槌打	Wankan	Sideways, iron hammer, hit or strike
Yoko Ude Hasami	横腕狭	Tekki Sandan	Side, arm, trapping,
Yumi Zuki	弓突	Sochin	Bow, strike
Zenkutsu Dachi	前屈立	Heian Shodan	Front bent, stance
Zenpo Enpi Uchi	前方猿臂打	Nijushiho	Forward bent, elbow, hit or strike

Index

CPSIA information can be obtained
at www.ICGtesting.com
Printed in the USA
LVHW021714050120

6425671LV00001B/53

9 781489 723529